Grace Saves All

Grace Saves All

The Necessity of Christian Universalism

David Artman

FOREWORD BY
Brad Jersak

AFTERWORD BY
Thomas Talbott

WIPF & STOCK · Eugene, Oregon

GRACE SAVES ALL
The Necessity of Christian Universalism

Copyright © 2020 David Artman. All rights reserved. Except for brief quotations in critical publications or reviews, no part of this book may be reproduced in any manner without prior written permission from the publisher. Write: Permissions, Wipf and Stock Publishers, 199 W. 8th Ave., Suite 3, Eugene, OR 97401.

Wipf & Stock
An Imprint of Wipf and Stock Publishers
199 W. 8th Ave., Suite 3
Eugene, OR 97401

www.wipfandstock.com

PAPERBACK ISBN: 978-1-5326-5088-8
HARDCOVER ISBN: 978-1-5326-5089-5
EBOOK ISBN: 978-1-5326-5090-1

All Scripture references are from the New International Version (NIV) unless otherwise noted.

Manufactured in the U.S.A.   04/06/20

For all those who struggle to find a God of true love,

and for my wife Amy,
who always knew it had to be so.

Contents

Foreword by Brad Jersak | ix
Introduction | xiii

Chapter 1—The Bible | 1
Chapter 2—Judgment | 20
Chapter 3—Grace | 31
Chapter 4—Hell | 46
Chapter 5—The Book of Revelation | 68
Chapter 6—Mystery and Free Will | 78
Chapter 7—Authenticity | 90
Chapter 8—My Story | 108

Conclusion | 117
Afterword by Thomas Talbott | 121
Acknowledgments | 127
Recommended Reading | 129
Appendix—Lenten Devotional 2018 | 139
Bibliography | 145

Foreword

Brad Jersak

THE WINDS HAVE CHANGED in modern eschatology—dramatically so. As an evangelical child of the "Jesus People" era and seventies revivalism, I was raised in a movement fixated on the end times. We were immersed in dispensationalism, the great tribulation, the identity of the antichrist and armies of Armageddon. We waited for an imminent second coming (probably next week) and final heaven or hell judgment. Along with a frankly cultic Left Behind obsession was this complete assumption that the unsaved at death were eternally doomed to eternal conscious torment in an actual lake of fire.

Today, those of us who've made our happy exit from the lunacy of blood moon prophecies and doomsday dates have been humbled (I hope) by embarrassment at our misplaced certainty. We've let go of much of our speculation about the how "the End" works. Most of all, the Infernalist monopoly on the nature of hell, who goes there, and for how long, has crumbled. New camps have arisen and secured a place at the discussion table. Alongside eternal conscious torment, a serious case is being made for alternative outcomes. Among these, the late great John Stott made it possible for Evangelicals to consider and embrace conditionalism (whether annihilation or conditional immortality). More dramatically, teachers like Robin Parry, David Bentley Hart, and Ilaria Ramelli have taken a bold stand for Christian universalism. And these aren't wishy-washy post-theistic liberals—they represent Nicene orthodoxy and have demanded we attend to those church fathers and mothers of old—most notably Gregory of Nyssa—and spiritual giants throughout the centuries, from the Moravian evangelists to George MacDonald to St. Silouan the Athonite. Their argument is that ultimate redemption is not a thin and popular novelty. It has deep historic roots in the ancient faith, even as a minority report.

In my view, two great errors must be avoided: (1) uninformed, knee-jerk charges of heresy and (2) the sloppy pop-universalism that fails to proclaim Christ alone, the necessity of a faith response, or the reality of judgment. In *Grace Saves All*, David Artman skillfully avoids both ditches. With careful ears, a thoughtful mind, and a wise voice, he's able to engage other points of view (even mine) with generosity and conviction.

While I don't track with all of Artman's arguments across the board, I find him biblically compelling and theologically orthodox. Indeed, he IS a friend and interlocutor with whom our iron-sharpening-iron engagement is marked by trust and bears good fruit.

My reasons for my own slow pace down the path he treads are twofold. First, I am still working out how to proclaim a broader hope in ways that don't license the Christless universalism I mentioned above. Sharing the truth of the good news of Jesus Christ should not cause those who let go of an endless hell to dismiss Christ along with it. And yet, somehow it does. Often. Something is off there. Did they really never know Christ? Did they simply follow him under threat of hell? Was their faith in hell rather than in Christ to begin with? So, from the time of Origen—a universalist for sure—teachings on ultimate redemption have been accompanied by this disturbing trend that made the great teachers hesitate out of pastoral concern for the immature. My problem with that is that offering a noble lie in place of a dangerous truth is not a solution. If it were, we'd have to abandon Paul's radical grace teaching. Alas, I don't yet have a good solution. But I suspect it has something to do with raising our Christology, delivering on the promise of authentic encounter, and maintaining a more intense theology of restorative judgment.

Second, I personally remain in the good company of "hopeful inclusivists" (St. Maximos the Confessor, Hans Urs von Balthasar, and Metropolitan Kallistos Ware) in their commitment in principle to God's costly reverence for human freedom, apart from which there can be no willing trust or authentic love. This "hope" should not be mistaken as "wishful" or "doubtful"—as the hymn says, "My hope is built on nothing less than Jesus' blood and righteousness." Mine is "the blessed Hope and glorious appearing of the great God and our Savior, Jesus Christ" (Titus 2:13). Like St. Gregory or Robin Parry, I believe the Bible foresees the willing turn of every last human being back toward the heart of the Father. And God's foreknowledge is not coercive or deterministic—he simply foresees and reveals our willing response (as in Phil 2 or 1 Cor 15).

At the end of the day, I hope, pray, and preach for God's will to be fulfilled, which the New Testament reveals is the salvation of all people and the restoration of all things. I hold ultimate redemption as a conviction—I just don't *presume* to teach it as doctrine.

In the case of David Artman, I detect no presumption. I see a man of faith who carefully combs and back-combs the Scriptures to test his best spiritual instincts in tandem with fellow pilgrims making our way home to the Abba's House. I commend his faithfulness to Christ and to this task.

Amor Vincit Omnia

Brad Jersak (PhD Theology)

Author of *Her Gates Will Never Be Shut* and *A More Christlike God*

Introduction

> Grace is the divine expedient designed to remedy
> the predicament of sin.
>
> —Jurgen Moltmann[1]

Grace is amazing. About this all Christians agree. Yet nearly all forms of Christianity put significant limits on grace. Those forms of Christianity which proclaim that grace alone actually saves typically don't believe God gives grace to everyone, while those forms of Christianity which proclaim God gives grace to everyone typically don't believe grace alone actually saves. Is the Christian understanding of grace necessarily divided between these two grace-limiting options? Must grace either be that which saves alone but doesn't go to all, or that which goes to all but doesn't save alone? Or, is there another way? Can one be Christian and understand grace to save alone *and* go to all? Can one be a Christian and believe salvation by grace alone is for everyone?

I will argue here that being Christian does not require one to limit either grace's power or scope. It's quite possible, I will contend, to be Christian *and* to believe grace is God's way of finally saving everyone. Grace can be understood to be God's remedy for all human sin, not just part of it. Grace can mean God perseveres with us until we've all seen the light and freely responded in faith. Grace can mean God is with us not just *if* we get things right, but *until* we get things right. How long it takes for us to get things right is not the primary issue for God. Whether it happens in this lifetime, or in the age to come, or in the ages to come after that, is not what

---

1. Moltmann, *Coming of God*, 262.

really matters.² The primary issue for God isn't how hard it will be for us, or how long it will take us. The primary issue for God is our final return home. And, like the father of the prodigal son, God will be vigilant until we all make our way home from the far country.

Even though I will be arguing here that everyone will finally be saved by grace alone, what we do still matters very much. We each still have our part to play. And neither will I be downplaying the consequences of sin. We are granted terrifying freedom to bring tremendous misery upon ourselves and others. What we do matters greatly. But no matter what we do, God's grace can be understood to include God's commitment to be with us, even in the form of judgment and hell, until we eventually see the light. I will argue that God's perfecting love is continually with all of us, through whatever hell may be necessary, until all of us are finally healed and home. What makes grace truly amazing is God never giving up and never failing—God being able to save even those for whom there is apparently no hope. I maintain that it's possible to be a Christian and to have this understanding of grace.

Unfortunately, most people don't know it's possible to be a Christian and to believe grace is God's way of ultimately saving everyone. They don't know where to find biblical evidence for this understanding of grace. They don't know this way of understanding grace was common in early Christianity. They wrongly assume they can only be Christian if they also believe God will not, or might not, save everyone. Through this book I hope to help correct these false impressions and assumptions.

This book also grows out of my experiences in pastoral ministry.³ Part of the job of a minister is to encourage ongoing spiritual growth. Over the years this responsibility forced me to grapple with two big questions: First, do we grow spiritually in order to make God love us more? And second, do we grow spiritually in order to somehow earn our salvation?⁴ As I have come to see it, we don't grow spiritually in order to make God

---

2. In Ephesians 2:7 Paul refers not just to a coming age, but to coming ages.

3. I am a minister in the Christian Church (Disciples of Christ). We are online at www.disciples.org. In our church each person forms their own theological opinions. We follow the old saying, "In essentials unity. In non-essentials liberty. And in all things love."

4. With regard to salvation, there is both a temporal (regarding the here and now) and an eschatological (regarding the eternal) dimension to it. When I use the term "salvation" in this book I will be referring primarily to its eschatological dimension. To put it in common terms, even though it is an oversimplification, salvation will be equated with whether or not a person is ultimately fully reconciled with God in eternity.

love us more. God loves us not because of who we are, but because of who God is. Since God is love, there's nothing we can do to make God love us more and nothing we can do to make God love us less. But if we don't grow spiritually to make God love us more, then do we grow spiritually to somehow earn our salvation? Again, I would have to say no. We don't grow spiritually in order to earn our salvation. We are saved by grace. The point of spiritual growth is not to earn salvation but to *experience* the salvation in which we've already been included by grace. Grace precedes and powers everything, including faith itself.

This brings us to the topic of grace, and it raises a central question for this book: if we are saved by grace, then *how* are we saved by grace? All Christians agree that salvation can't occur without grace. Yet, all Christians do not agree about the role grace plays *in* salvation. When I look over the history of Christianity, I see three basic approaches which have been taken on this issue of how grace saves. In order to easily distinguish between each of these three approaches, I assign each a broad term.

I give the term *Transactional* to the first approach because it sees salvation as being a two-part process which takes place between God and people.[5] There's God's part (grace) and there's the human part (that which is beyond grace). If people do enough of their part then the result is salvation. If not, then salvation is lost. Even though everyone gets grace, grace by itself does not guarantee salvation. There's a part of salvation which is finally left up to each person, and God's grace doesn't ensure the accomplishment of this remaining part. In the Transactional approach, grace goes to all, but grace alone doesn't actually save.

I assign the term *Exclusive* to the second approach because it sees salvation as being exclusively for some and not for others. In this approach those whom God chooses to save are called *the elect*, and salvation is exclusively for them. God excludes all the rest from even the possibility of salvation. In the Exclusive approach salvation is not something humans achieve with God. It's something God achieves with humans. Salvation is not a two-part process. It's a one-part process in that God's part assures that everything necessary for the other part of salvation will finally come to pass. No transaction is involved. Sinners, who are understood to be dead in sin, don't do anything to recommend themselves to God. God makes sure that for the elect salvation is always initiated, sustained, and completed. God keeps working with

---

5. The idea of thinking of spirituality as a transaction was first suggested to me by Rob Bell in an episode of his podcast. Bell, "Alternative Wisdom," 24:49.

the elect until they are able to do everything necessary for salvation. The elect are the only ones saved, and their salvation is accomplished by grace alone. In the Exclusive approach, grace alone actually saves, but since saving grace doesn't go to all, everyone is not saved.

I use the term *Inclusive* for the third approach to how grace saves because it sees salvation as being neither transactional nor exclusive. This approach is non-transactional because salvation is based completely on God's choice to initiate and to guarantee that all things necessary for salvation will finally come to pass. It's non-exclusive in that no one is excluded from being one of the persons God intends to save. Being included in salvation is something that's for everyone—no exceptions. The Inclusive approach agrees with the Transactional approach about grace going to all, and it agrees with the Exclusive approach about grace alone actually being able to save. Therefore, in the Inclusive approach, everyone is eventually saved by grace alone.

The Transactional, Exclusive, and Inclusive approaches (as I define those terms here) are all part of the history of Christianity. All are being practiced today. They are all possible ways of being Christian. However, people are generally unaware of the Inclusive approach. They assume being Christian means being part of a spirituality which is in some way either transactional or exclusive. However, I've seen that when people find out about an inclusive Christian spirituality which is neither transactional nor exclusive, it can open the door to Christian faith for them. And then, when they find out about a church which allows the Inclusive approach, it can open the door to Christian fellowship for them as well.

When I first conceived of this book my purpose was mainly to increase awareness of, and to make a case for, the Inclusive approach. However, through the process of research and writing, it became increasingly clear to me that something much more was at stake. The core conviction I reached was that the Inclusive approach is not just one approach to Christian theology—it is the *only* approach to Christian theology which can successfully defend the goodness of God; and therein lies its necessity. As I will argue, it is not possible to successfully defend the goodness of an all-knowing and all-powerful God unless the salvation this all-knowing and all-powerful God achieves is also all-inclusive in scope.

It is this universal scope of salvation which God achieves in the Inclusive approach that accounts for the reason it is variously called universal reconciliation, universal salvation, or perhaps most accurately, Christian universalism. Although I did not originally intend to write a book which made such a pointed case for the necessity of the Inclusive/Christian universalist approach, that's where my journey has taken me. It would be disingenuous for me to suggest otherwise, or to hide my ultimate findings for fear they are too bold.

Having disclosed the ultimate end of my argument, let me now lay out how the book unfolds from the beginning. The Foreword by Brad Jersak sets the stage by showing how this is a dynamic time in which there is much reevaluation of Christian thinking about eternal destinies. Chapter 1 presents a basic five-point biblical theology for the Inclusive approach. Chapter 2 examines a biblical view of judgment which is consistent with it. Chapter 3 explores how the relationship between grace and salvation is handled in each of the three approaches, as well as pointing out the difficulties the Transactional and Exclusive approaches face in defending God's goodness. Chapter 4 addresses how the Inclusive approach handles the concept of hell. Chapter 5 proposes an inclusive approach to reading of the book of Revelation. Chapter 6 deals with the twin challenges of mystery and free will, describes the option of hopeful inclusivism, and then goes on to argue for the necessity of moving beyond hopeful inclusivism to a confident Christian universalism. Chapter 7 presents the Inclusive approach as both an ancient and modern expression of the Christian faith, as well as further defends its necessity in order to preserve the goodness of God. The Conclusion summarizes the book's arguments and provides recommendations for further reading. An Afterword by Christian philosopher Thomas Talbott, a leading expert on Christian universalism, adds further logical clarity to the conversation. After that comes my acknowledgments, recommendations for further reading, and an appendix which contains the text of a sermon I gave on this subject, as well as a link to a YouTube video of it.

Can God's offer of grace be both non-transactional and non-exclusive? Could it be that God will ultimately redeem all? Is it possible to be a Christian *and* to believe that grace is God's way of finally saving everyone? As a Christian, is it possible to engage in spiritual growth which is in no way driven by the fear of eternal rejection? Could it be that the God of Christianity is not only all-powerful and all-knowing, but also all-good? Could it be that grace saves all? I believe the answer to all of these questions is yes.

1

The Bible

> If the truth itself (and not an elaborate deception) is what ultimately sets us free, then that tells us something important about the nature of the truth. It tells us that the truth about the universe is ultimately glorious, not tragic; it is something God can gladly reveal to us, not something he must conceal from us forever, lest it undermine our happiness in the end.
>
> —Thomas Talbott[1]

A Five-Point Theology for the Inclusive Approach

IN THE INTRODUCTION I argued for an Inclusive approach to Christian theology which understands grace to be God's way of saving everyone. If grace is, in fact, God's way of saving everyone, then the truth about the universe is ultimately glorious, and not tragic. We are all included. None of us will finally be lost, and the goodness of God will finally prevail in the lives of every person. Now I will lay out a five-point biblical framework for this Inclusive approach in which all are saved. Taken together, these five points outline a picture of an utterly good God whose goodness will finally permeate all. The five points of this approach are:[2]

---

1. Talbott, *Inescapable Love of God*, 181.
2. Some may observe that one might well "prove" anything from the Bible by drawing upon certain proof-text passages. It is true that biblical interpretation is more complicated than simply trotting out a few Scriptures and pronouncing that, "The Bible says . . ." Over the course of this book I hope to show that the Inclusive approach is grounded in a legitimate reading of the Bible, that this reading fits best with the character of God revealed in Christ, and also that it provides the only narrative arc which satisfactorily fits with the doctrine of an all-good, all-powerful, and all-knowing God.

1. God is a loving parent to all.
2. God sincerely wants to save all.
3. God, in Christ, covers the sin of all.
4. God is sovereign over all.
5. God will be all in all.

These five points move in a certain order. They begin with this fundamental assertion: God has a loving parental relationship with everyone. Arising out of this parental love comes the next point: God sincerely desires the salvation of each person. The way God accomplishes this salvation is addressed in the next point: God, in Christ, covers the sin of all. The fourth point—God is sovereign over all—highlights the sovereign power of God, which enables God both to foresee everything God sincerely desires, and then to forestall anything which might thwart it. The final point—God will be all in all—looks forward to God ultimately being fully reconciled with each one of God's own dear children. Having outlined each of these points, we now examine some of the ways each of them finds support in the Bible.

The First Point—God Is a Loving Parent to All

God loves each and every person in just the same way as a good parent loves a dear child. The following Scriptures point in the direction of a God who eternally loves each person with this kind of love:

> 1 John 4:8—Whoever does not love does not know God, because God is love.

> 1 Corinthians 13:4-8—Love is patient; love is kind; love is not envious or boastful or arrogant or rude. It does not insist on its own way; it is not irritable or resentful; it does not rejoice in wrongdoing, but rejoices in the truth. It bears all things, believes all things, hopes all things, endures all things. Love never ends.

> Matthew 5:43-45—You have heard that it was said, "You shall love your neighbor and hate your enemy." But I say to you, Love your enemies and pray for those who persecute you, so that you may be children of your Father in heaven.

Acts 17:27-29—God . . . is not far from any one of us. 'For in him we live and move and have our being.' As some of your own poets have said, 'We are his offspring.' "Therefore, since we are God's offspring we should not think that the divine being is like gold or silver or stone—an image made by human design and skill.

Ephesians 3:14-15—For this reason I kneel before the Father, from whom every family in heaven and on earth derives its name.

Ephesians 4:6— . . . one God and Father of all, who is over all and through all and in all.

Consider what these biblical texts have to say about the nature of God's love. In 1 John 4:8 we are not just told God loves, but that God *is* love. Love is not just one part of God's nature, but the essence of God's nature. This means God's love is not coerced or forced. God freely loves out of the deepest essence of God's own being. Love is not what motivates God at certain moments and then not at others. Whatever God is doing is always necessarily rooted in God's essential character as love.

The passage from 1 Corinthians 13 gives us a biblical definition of love in which love bears all things, believes all things, hopes all things, endures all things, and never ends. When we apply this definition of love to God, and then to the way God acts in love toward each soul, we may arrive at the following conclusions: God loves each soul. God bears all for each soul. God believes all for each soul. God hopes all for each soul. God endures all for each soul. And, since love never ends, we can infer God's redemptive efforts towards each soul are never-ending as well. If God's love corresponds to Paul's description of love as seen in 1 Corinthians 13, then God's love towards each of us is constant. God loves us in this way because it is in God's nature to do so. There's nothing we can do to make God love us more. There's nothing we can do to make God love us less.

In the passage from Matthew 5 Jesus teaches his followers to love their enemies because in so doing they are reflecting their Father in heaven who does the same. Loving enemies, in the eyes of Jesus, is not just right in theory. It is right because it is what the Father in heaven does. As we go about loving enemies we are being "sons of" the Father. The lesson we learn here is not only that we should love enemies, but also that God is an enemy lover—because when someone loves their enemies, they are doing what God does.

The passage taken from Acts 17 is part of a speech given by the apostle Paul to the people of Athens. Notice the spiritual problem Paul addressed in this speech. The problem Paul faced was not *how* to make the people of ancient Athens into God's children. That's because, according to what Paul says in this passage, they *already were* God's children. They already had a parental relationship with God. Closeness to the loving parent-God was not something which they had to achieve. Notice also how Paul regarded their status as God's children to be so obviously established that even their own pagan poets knew about it. The challenge Paul faced with the people of Athens lay in finding a way to help them realize that God was *already* close to each one of them, that God was *already* their parent in whom they were living and moving and having their being. From Paul's point of view, the spiritual problem for the people of Athens was not their distance *from* God, but their disinformation *about* God. Because they didn't know any better, they worshiped a distant God through their idols and their temples. But now, according to Paul, the good news about God had been perfectly revealed in Jesus. Being close to God and becoming a child of God was not something they had to achieve. God was already near to them. God had already included them. They were already God's own children.

In the passage from Ephesians 3 we find out that the Father, literally the *Patera*, is the one from whom every family, literally every *patria*, derives its name. As David Bentley Hart notes, this means that every lineage, or family, or people, or tribe is "derived from a single forefather. The point here is that every family, clan, or people ultimately derives its lineage from the one God who is the Father of all."[3] In the passage from Ephesians 4 God is described as the totally encompassing Father of all, who is not only over all, but who is also through all and in all.

Putting all of these passages of Scripture together suggests a God whose total essence is love; who is close to each person; in whom each person lives, moves, and has their being; who loves even enemies; who regards each person as a precious child; and who is over, and through, and in all. This means nobody has to complete a spiritual transaction in order to become a valuable child of God because they already are. This means nobody has to be chosen in order to make God be close to them, because God already is.

---

3. Hart, *The New Testament*, 383.

The Second Point—God Sincerely Wants to Save All

Everyone is already included among those God sincerely wants to save. Saying God *sincerely* desires the salvation of all means God is bound and determined to be victorious with each one of us. The following Scripture passages show how it is God's determined purpose for all people to be included in, and to benefit from, salvation:

> Genesis 12:3—[spoken by God to Abraham] ". . . all peoples on earth will be blessed through you."

> Ezekiel 33:11—Say to them, "As surely as I live, declares the Sovereign LORD, I take no pleasure in the death of the wicked, but rather that they turn from their ways and live."

> John 12:32—"And I, when I am lifted up from the earth, will draw all people to myself."

> Luke 15:4–7—"Which one of you, having a hundred sheep and losing one of them, does not leave the ninety-nine in the wilderness and go after the one that is lost until he finds it? When he has found it, he lays it on his shoulders and rejoices. And when he comes home, he calls together his friends and neighbors, saying to them, 'Rejoice with me, for I have found my sheep that was lost.'"

> 1 Timothy 2:3–4—God our Savior . . . desires everyone to be saved and to come to the knowledge of the truth.

> 2 Peter 3:9—The Lord is not slow in keeping his promise, as some understand slowness. Instead he is patient with you, not wanting anyone to perish, but everyone to come to repentance.

This set of Scriptures shows how God sincerely wants all people to be saved. In the Genesis passage Abraham is told that in him, or through him, all the families of the earth shall be blessed. God's elect people, called into existence through Abraham and Sarah, were to become the vehicles through which God would bless the whole world. They were to be a conduit of grace, not a cul-de-sac. In the passage from John 12 we see the same intention to bless all people through Jesus, whose ministry was an extension of the ministry of blessing God started through Abraham.

In the passage from John 12 Jesus speaks of drawing all people to himself. The word translated as "draw" is a form of the Greek verb *helkuo*. The verb *helkuo* implies a determined, resolute action. For example, a form of *helkuo* is used in John 18 to describe how Peter drew his sword and then used it to cut off the ear of the high priest's servant when Jesus was being arrested. Another example is found John 21 where a form of *helkuo* is also used to describe what is happening when the disciples drag a net completely full of fish to Jesus. Keeping the meaning of *helkuo* in mind, when we read John 12:32, where Jesus speaks of drawing all people to himself after being lifted up, we can think of a man resolutely drawing a sword, or of a fisherman straining to drag in a net full of fish. Implied in these actions is a determined pulling, a sincere commitment to see the task at hand through until it is completed. John 12:32 demonstrates the sincere and determined will of Jesus to draw all people to himself for their salvation. This shows us how Jesus, and by extension God, is not passive with regard to people coming to him and his salvation.

Luke 15:4–7 shows how every single one of the shepherd's sheep is precious and how not even a single one is expendable. The shepherd goes searching until he finds the lost one. In the Greek of the New Testament a form of the verb *apollumi*, meaning destroyed or cut off, is used to describe the lost state of the sheep. However, when a sheep is found it is no longer destroyed. This is important to understand in Jesus' parables in Luke 15 about the lost sheep, the lost coin, and the lost son. The sheep, coin, and son are all described with a form of the word *apollumi*, the same word which is associated with destruction elsewhere in the New Testament. We should keep the nature of *apollumi* in mind when reading passages which describe the destruction to which sin leads. In the Bible when someone experiences judgment which leads to destruction it is a very, very serious thing, but it does not necessarily imply an absolute annihilation. The lost sheep was destroyed when it was lost and then undestroyed when it was found. The same went for the lost coin and the lost son. And the situation of the lost son was even more extreme than that of the sheep and the coin—for the lost son was not only thought of as being lost, but also as being dead. When the lost son came back home, the father understood him to be more than just found. He had been dead and now he was alive again. Therefore, the state of lostness described by *apollumi* can imply even death. But even the lostness and deadness of *apollumi* is not irreversible with God.

The passages from Ezekiel 33, 1 Timothy, and 2 Peter also tell us God desires everyone to be saved and for none to perish. In Ezekiel 33 we read about the God who takes no delight in the death of the wicked, but would rather they turn from their evil ways and live. In 1 Timothy God is described as one who desires everyone to be saved and to come to the knowledge of truth. In 2 Peter we learn God does not want anyone to perish. In other words, nobody's expendable. Nobody's loss can be acceptable to the God who wants all to be saved and none to perish. As Robin Parry notes, "The claim that God does not love and wish to save all is a very hard pill for the Christian to swallow. It seems to entail a denial of the claim that God's nature is to love his creatures (as 1 John 4:8, 16b seems to teach), that Christ died for all people (as 1 John 2:2 seems to teach), and that God desires to save all (as 2 Pet 3:9, 1 Tim 2:4, and Ezekiel 33:11 seem to teach). According to theists, God is the greatest possible being. In light of the biblical emphasis on the supreme value of love, it seems plausible to think that a being that loves *all* is greater than a being who loves some but not others."[4]

When we combine the implications of all these passages a picture emerges of a loving God who really does sincerely desire for all people to be saved. There is not one lost child God wants to stay lost. It is God's purpose for all who are lost to be found in Christ. God does not want any prodigal child to be destroyed forever. There is no condition which must be fulfilled in order to be qualified. God unconditionally elects everyone to be included among those God sincerely desires to save.

The Third Point—God, in Christ, Covers the Sin of All

God, in Christ, has established a covering of righteousness which includes and shelters everyone, not just a limited group of elect people. Everyone is caught up and covered in the saving effects of Jesus' incarnation, crucifixion, and resurrection. No one is excluded, and no spiritual transaction must be completed in order to make it effective. The following biblical texts demonstrate this:

> Romans 5:18—Therefore just as one man's trespass led to condemnation for all, so one man's act of righteousness leads to justification and life for all.
>
> 2 Corinthians 5:14—For the love of Christ urges us on, because we are convinced that one has died for all; therefore all have died.
>
> Colossians 3:3—For you died, and your life is now hidden with Christ in God.

---

4. MacDonald, *Evangelical Universalist*, 20.

> 1 John 2:2—... he is the atoning sacrifice for our sins, and not for ours only but also for the sins of the whole world.
>
> 1 Timothy 2:5–6—For there is one God and one mediator between God and mankind, the man Christ Jesus, who gave himself as a ransom for all people.
>
> 2 Corinthians 5:19—... God was reconciling the world to himself in Christ, not counting people's sins against them.

These Scriptures demonstrate the inclusive nature of what God has done in Christ. In Romans 5:18 Paul contrasts the disobedience of Adam (which leads to condemnation and death for all) with the obedience of Christ (which leads to justification and life for all). Nobody had to make a transaction or be chosen in order to be affected by Adam. Nobody had to make a transaction or be chosen in order to be affected by Christ. Because of Adam, everyone was incorporated into sin and death. Because of Christ, everyone was incorporated into righteousness and life. What happened with Adam was inclusive, and to everyone's detriment. What happened with Christ was also inclusive, but to everyone's benefit.

Second Corinthians 5:14 shows how all have been included in the death of Christ. Here we are told Jesus has died for all, therefore all have died. When Jesus died, all of humanity died with him. Nobody had to ask or be chosen in order to be included in the death of Christ. They were included because they were human. In Colossians 3:3 we are told dying in Christ results in having one's life hidden in Christ with God. If Christ has died for all, and if all have been included in Christ because of it, then is not all of humanity, in effect, hidden in Christ? This was the line of reasoning followed by Karl Barth (1886–1968), one of the most influential theologians of the twentieth century. About this universal inclusion in Christ, Barth wrote, "In Christian doctrine ... we have always to take in blind seriousness the basic Pauline perception of Colossians 3:3 which is that of all Scripture—that our life is hid with Christ in God. With Christ: never at all apart from him, never at all independently of him, never at all in and for itself. We as human beings never at all exist in ourselves ... We exist as human beings in Jesus Christ and in him alone; as we also find God in Jesus Christ and in him alone."[5] George Hunsinger, a scholar of Barth's theology, neatly summarizes Barth's understanding of humanity's universal incorporation into Christ:

---

5. Hunsinger, *How to Read Karl Barth*, 37–38.

What Barth says about God's objective self-involvement in Jesus Christ finds a remarkable parallel in what Barth says with respect to humanity. For humanity, too, is conceived as objectively self-involved in Jesus Christ in a manner at once hidden and revealed. Just as God is ontologically present in Jesus Christ, so too is the human race ontologically present in him in the sense that in and only in him is its own true reality to be found. Christian theology has traditionally emphasized that God comes to the human race in Jesus Christ. Barth shares that emphasis, but goes on to develop an extraordinary anthropological correlate. When God comes to humanity in the history of Jesus Christ, humanity at the same time is brought to God in that history objectively. *It is not faith which incorporates humanity into Jesus Christ. Faith is rather the acknowledgment of a mysterious incorporation already objectively accomplished on humanity's behalf.*[6]

As George Hunsinger points out, for Karl Barth, Colossians 3:3 captured the basic scriptural truth of humanity's mysterious incorporation into Christ. This points us further towards understanding how we are included or hidden in Christ through no effort of our own. Our inclusion is accomplished for us in a sovereign act of God. Faith is not what incorporates us into Christ. Faith is what makes us aware of and able to act upon our already accomplished incorporation into Christ.

The passage from 1 John proclaims Christ as the atoning sacrifice for the whole world, not just for part of the world. Jesus did not go to the cross for the benefit of some, but for the benefit of all. In similar fashion, the 1 Timothy passage announces Jesus as the ransom for all people, not just for some people. As all people are held hostage by sin and death, so Jesus pays the ransom price for all. Humanity was unable to pay the ransom, so Jesus payed it for humanity. In so doing, Jesus set all humanity free.

All of this is done without humanity having to do anything. Nobody had to have faith in Adam in order to be included in the negative consequences which came from Adam's disobedience. Nobody had to accept Adam into their life in order to be included in Adam's sin. In the same way, nobody had to have faith in Jesus in order to be included in the positive consequences which came through Jesus' obedience. Just as Adam covered humanity in guilt, even more so, Jesus covered humanity's guilt with his own perfect righteousness. The universal sin of Adam was covered by the universal atonement of Christ. This is how we have all been included in the

---

6. Hunsinger, *How to Read Karl Barth*, 38. Emphasis mine.

righteousness of Christ. This is all summed up by Paul's declaration in 2 Corinthians 5:9 that, in Christ, God was reconciling the world to himself. Robin Parry, writing under the pen name of Gregory MacDonald at the time, referred to this verse in his summation of the work of Christ:

> ... in Jesus Christ God has acted to save Israel and, thus, to save the world. On the cross he takes upon himself Israel's exile and Humanity's expulsion, both conceived in terms of a divine curse. His resurrection anticipates the return from exile the Jews longed for and the restoration of humanity and creation. Christ is thus, on the one hand, the Messiah representing the nation of Israel and, on the other, the second Adam representing the whole of humanity. In his representative role nobody is excluded. Christ's death is not merely on behalf of some elect grouping within the wider family of humanity. He represented all, and his death was for all without any exceptions. In his resurrection, the whole of creation is reconciled, and the whole of humanity is redeemed. None of this makes participation in redemption automatic—repentance and faith are necessary responses to grace. Paul still urges his hearers to be reconciled to God immediately after declaring that God was in Christ reconciling the world to himself (2 Cor. 5:18–20).[7]

As Parry points out, God, in Christ, accomplished the reconciliation of the world to himself, but the working out of that reconciliation still has to take place over time. The reconciliation accomplished in Christ created a covering of forgiveness for all humanity, but the full transformation taking place under that covering will only be realized in the coming ages. This transformation requires our participation and God's power in order for it to all finally take place.

The Fourth Point—God Is Sovereign Over All

God will prevail in God's will because God is sovereign. To affirm the sovereignty of God is to affirm that God, being supremely powerful, is able to achieve everything God wants to achieve within the realm where God is sovereignly in charge. If God is love, and if God is sovereign, then God is sovereign love. To affirm this is to affirm God's will and God's love as the most powerful forces in the lives of each and every person. To affirm the sovereignty of God over each human life is to affirm God's ultimate

---

7. MacDonald, *The Evangelical Universalist*, 105.

authority over each of our eternal destinies. The following Biblical passages highlight the sovereignty of God:

> 2 Chronicles 20:6—O Lord, God of our ancestors, are you not God in heaven? Do you not rule over all the kingdoms of the nations? In your hand are power and might, so that no one is able to withstand you.
>
> Psalm 115:3—Our God is in the heavens; he does whatever he pleases.
>
> Psalm 135:6—Whatever the Lord pleases he does, in heaven and on earth, in the seas and all deeps.
>
> Proverbs 19:21—The human mind may devise many plans, but it is the purpose of the Lord that will be established.
>
> Job 42:2—"I know that you can do all things, and that no purpose of yours can be thwarted."
>
> Isaiah 14:24—The Lord Almighty has sworn, "Surely, as I have planned, so it will be, and as I have purposed, so it will happen."
>
> Isaiah 46:10— . . . declaring the end from the beginning and from ancient times things not yet done, saying, "My purpose shall stand, and I will fulfill my intention."
>
> Jeremiah 32:27— See, I am the Lord, the God of all flesh; is anything too hard for me?
>
> Matthew 19:26—But Jesus looked at them and said, "For mortals it is impossible, but for God all things are possible."
>
> Ephesians 1:11— . . . having been predestined according to the plan of him who works out everything in conformity with the purpose of his will.

Note in these passages how God is not only completely in charge, but also, according to Isaiah 46:10, the one who knows the end from the beginning. God is able to accomplish everything laid out in God's plan. God has designed everything which will come to pass, and no force or power is able to finally frustrate God's plans. God will not be surprised with the ultimate outcome of God's creation. The plan of God will ultimately be fully realized. Since there is seemingly no question about whether or not God knows about and is able to accomplish all God wants to accomplish, the main question then becomes, "What is it that God wants to accomplish?"

The sovereignty of God means God is in charge of everyone's ultimate destiny. As Proverbs 19 asserts, humans may devise many plans, but it is God's purpose which will finally be established. To affirm the sovereignty of God over all human life is to affirm we are already in the place where God is sovereign. The sovereignty of God, as a concept, brings tremendous theological repercussions along with it. Contemplating the full meaning of God's sovereignty can cause a complete theological overhaul. Once someone fully grasps the concept that God knows the end from the beginning and is not controlled or regulated by any outside forces, the following realization strikes home—the outcome of all things will inevitably be what God intended from the beginning. It means we as individuals and we as the human race are not ultimately in control. We are along for the ride, so to speak, and wherever that ride is going is not up to us. The following excerpt from Jen Hatmaker, in her book *Of Mess and Moxie*, is a good example of what can happen when a sincere Christian thoughtfully works through the bold implications of God's sovereignty:

> As for those sovereignty questions, I am sorry to say I don't exactly understand how it all works this side of heaven. I'm just not sure. . . . I can tell you what I make of the end game—I believe God's sovereignty ultimately means He will have it all back. Every wrong will eventually be right. Every injustice will be overturned. Every tear will be dried. All the torn pieces will be rewoven. Every prayer utilized to bring us another inch closer to Jesus and more in partnership with His love. This earth and realm will be repossessed into glory, and God will have the world He dreamed of. Some redemption will be in our lifetime, and all of it will be in eternity. Sovereignty means none of this is too far gone; nothing is outside God's ultimate plans. No matter how off the rails this world appears, God's eye has always been on the tiny, fragile sparrow. He has never lost count of an injustice, a life, a human being. No nameless death was ever nameless. No senseless abuse was ever missed. He may have set the whole earth in motion with its mix of humanity and spiritual realms and principalities, but only One is on the throne where He has always been and will always be. If we are still holding a pile of tattered threads, it just means the story is not over yet. We can trust God entirely until heaven when He vanquishes all tears, all death, all mourning, all crying, all pain, and He reigns and He won and He fixed it all and saved it all and restored it all.[8]

8. Hatmaker, *Of Mess and Moxie*, 250.

These kinds of conclusions are unavoidable when one fully appreciates the implications of believing in an all-knowing, all-good, all-powerful, completely sovereign God. All of this implies a grace which is finally triumphant, and an endgame in which everyone is restored. Therefore, we should expect to see an indication of this in the Scriptures, and this takes us to the last point—God will finally be all in all.

The Fifth Point—God Will Be All in All

The ultimate goal of God is to be fully present in each of our lives so that we might become fully illuminated and exist in complete harmony with God, others, and all of creation. The ultimate purpose of God is not for us to be merely forgiven, merely excused from punishment. God's final goal is for us to become fully aware, fully alive, and fully integrated into the perfect love of the Father, Son, and Spirit. In this way God will finally be all in all, and therefore, love will finally be all in all. The following biblical passages point in this direction:

> 1 Corinthians 15:28—When all things are subjected to him, then the Son himself will also be subjected to the one who put all things in subjection under him, so that God may be all in all.

> Romans 11:32—For God has imprisoned all in disobedience so that he may be merciful to all.

> Ephesians 1:9–10— . . . he has made known to us the mystery of his will, according to his good pleasure that he set forth in Christ, as a plan for the fullness of time, to gather up all things in him, things in heaven and things on earth.

> Psalm 22:28–30—All the ends of the earth will remember and turn to the Lord, and all the families of the nations will bow down before him, for dominion belongs to the Lord and he rules over the nations. All the rich of the earth will feast and worship; all who go down to the dust will kneel before him—those who cannot keep themselves alive.

> Isaiah 45:23—By myself I have sworn, my mouth has uttered in all integrity a word that will not be revoked: Before me every knee will bow; by me every tongue will swear.

Romans 14:11—For it is written, "As I live, says the Lord, every knee shall bow to me, and every tongue shall give praise to God."

Philippians 2:9–11—Therefore God also highly exalted him and gave him the name that is above every name, so that at the name of Jesus every knee should bend, in heaven and on earth and under the earth, and every tongue should confess that Jesus Christ is Lord, to the glory of God the Father.

Colossians 1:16–20— . . . for in him all things in heaven and on earth were created, things visible and invisible, whether thrones or dominions or rulers or powers—all things have been created through him and for him. He himself is before all things, and in him all things hold together. He is the head of the body, the church; he is the beginning, the firstborn from the dead, so that he might come to have first place in everything. For in him all the fullness of God was pleased to dwell, and through him God was pleased to reconcile to himself all things, whether on earth or in heaven, by making peace through the blood of his cross.

1 John 3:8—The Son of God was revealed for this purpose, to destroy the works of the devil.

Acts 3:21—"Heaven must receive him until the time comes for God to restore everything, as he promised long ago through his holy prophets."

Matthew 17:11—Jesus replied, "To be sure, Elijah comes and will restore all things."

Matthew 19:28—Jesus said to them, "Truly I tell you, at the renewal of all things, when the Son of Man sits on his glorious throne, you who have followed me will also sit on twelve thrones, judging the twelve tribes of Israel."

The passages above give us a sense of how the ultimate purpose of God's sovereign love is an all-inclusive, universal restoration of everything lost in the fall of creation from its original goodness. As Romans 11:32 informs us, God's purpose in imprisoning all in disobedience was to ultimately show mercy to all. Jan Bonda (1918–1997), after a lifetime of ministry in the Dutch Reformed Church, finally came to see how Paul's argument in Romans led to this conclusion. In his book *The One Purpose of God*, Bonda wrote, "Romans 11:32 is the finale of Paul's unfolding of the gospel, in which he summarizes his entire argument: All people have become disobedient, and all will find mercy with God."[9] The famous British New Testament scholar and theologian C.H. Dodd (1884–1973) reached a similar conclusion. In his commentary on the book of Romans, Dodd argued that Romans 11:32 pointed in the direction of a universal salvation. About this he wrote:

> . . . the final aim of [God in consigning all men to disobedience] is a state in which God's mercy is as universally effective as sin has been. In other words, it is the will of God that all mankind shall ultimately be saved.
> It has been thought incredible that Paul should have committed himself to such an absolute 'universalism.' But . . . he may be allowed to have meant what he said it its full sense: that God would *have mercy upon all*. If we really believe in One God, and believe that Jesus Christ, in what He was and what He did, truly shows what God's character and His attitude towards men are like, then it is very difficult to think ourselves out of the belief that somehow His love will find a way of bringing all men into unity with Him.[10]

Other biblical passages lead us to envision a universal reconciliation between God and humanity. First Corinthians 15:28 tells us God will finally be all in all. Psalm 22:28–30, Isaiah 45:23, and Romans 14:11 all look forward to the time when every knee will bow and every tongue confess. And if we look carefully at the Romans 14:11 passage we can see an indication that this confession won't be a begrudging one, but a glad one. The Greek verb *exomologestai* is used in this verse, and this verb not only means open confession and acknowledgment, but also glad praise, fullest thanks, and joyful proclamation.[11] And so David Bentley Hart, in his translation of the New Testament renders this verse, "For it has been written, '"As I live," says the Lord, "every knee shall bow to me, and every tongue shall *joyfully* praise God."'"[12]

About this future time when all will joyfully confess their glad allegiance, Thomas Talbott comments, "According to the New Testament as a whole, therefore, God sent his Son in the flesh, not as a conquering

---

9. Bonda, *One Purpose of God*, 192.
10. Dodd, *Epistle of Paul to the Romans*, 183–86. Emphasis original.
11. Hart, *The New Testament*, 319. Emphasis mine.
12. Hart, *The New Testament*, 314.

hero, but as a suffering servant; and the power that Jesus unleashed as he bled on the cross was precisely the power of self-giving love, the power to overcome evil by transforming the wills and renewing the minds of the evil ones themselves. The cross thus brings true peace, the kind that springs from within and requires reconciliation in the full redemptive sense. And because Paul also endorsed this idea . . . he seems clearly to have envisioned a time when all persons would be reconciled to God in the full redemptive sense."[13] In other words, there is a coming time envisioned in which everyone will happily acknowledge the salvation of God which has come through Christ.

Further, according to 1 John 3:8 the devil's work will be destroyed by the Son of God. If the devil's work is to break the relationship between God and people, then God's work is to restore it. And in the first chapter of Colossians we find the idea of Jesus being the one who reverses all that was lost in the fall. Colossians 1:16–20 proclaims Christ as the ultimate source of all creation and of all reconciliation. He is one through whom both everything is created and everything is reconciled. Once this happens, the time when everything will be restored, as described in Acts 3:21, will be at hand. The word translated as "restore" in Acts 3:21 is the Greek word *apokatastasis*. In the history of Christian theology, *apokatastasis* came to be the word associated with the belief that God would eventually return the creation back to the goodness of its original order.

Ilaria Ramelli, in her epic study entitled *The Christian Doctrine of Apokatastasis*, traces the development of this idea of a full restoration from its biblical origins through the early church fathers. At the end of her study she concludes,

> The doctrine of apokatastasis, as is found . . . in many Christian texts and Patristic authors, is a Christian doctrine and is grounded in Christ. . . . Indeed, the Christian doctrine of apokatastasis is based on the incarnation, death, and resurrection of Christ, and on God's being the supreme good. . . . The apokatastasis doctrine is historically very far from having been produced by an isolated character, excessively influenced or even "contaminated" by Greek theories, such as Origen has long considered to be. The apokatastasis doctrine is embedded in a much broader tradition, which is rooted in the New Testament itself and, even back, in some Jewish universalistic expectations, as I have argued.[14]

13. Talbott, *Inescapable Love of God*, 66.
14. Ramelli, *Christian Doctrine of Apokatastasis*, 817.

Ramelli, in her studies on this doctrine of the restoration of all things, also finds this restoration alluded to by Jesus in the passage from Matthew 17. Ramelli observes,

> One of the most interesting passages is Matthew 17:11, which is situated immediately after the Transfiguration, where Moses and Elijah had appeared as representatives of the Law and the Prophets respectively. Jesus is asked by his disciples whether Elijah will come before the Messiah at the end of times, as is prophesied in Malachi 3:23. He answers, "Elijah will indeed come and *apokatastesei panta*" (Matthew 17:11). The Vulagate renders: *Elias quidem venturus est, et restitute omnia.* Neither in the Greek nor in Latin is it clear that Elijah performs this restoration. It is not Elijah who will restore all beings in the end, at Christ's return, but God. As a prophet, Elijah will announce, indicate, and prepare, but the restoration of all will be a work of God.[15]

And so, as Ramelli argues, it is possible to see a connection between the Old Testament and the New Testament regarding a future restoration of all things.

In the Greek language the word *apokatastasis* could be applied to a variety of situations in which there was a return to original order. Greek astronomers used it to refer to the way the stars returned to their original position at the end of each year. Greek physicians used it to describe the healing and the return of the body to health. In politics it referred to the return to order after a season of tyranny.[16] The Jewish philosopher Philo (20 BC–AD 50) used the word to describe "the perfect and complete re-establishment of [the soul's] virtue."[17] As several early church fathers noted, and as several modern scholars corroborate, there is a sense in the Scriptures that the plan of God is the ultimate *apokatastasis* of humanity. This hope was more apparent to the early church fathers who read the New Testament in their native Greek tongue and who were not constrained by the restrictive church dogma which would develop later on, especially in the Latin-speaking church in the Western world. For the purposes of this book, the discussion of *apokatastasis* will be limited in scope to the restoration of humanity to its original harmony with God.[18]

---

15. Ramelli, *Christian Doctrine of Apokatastasis*, 11.

16. Ramelli, *Christian Doctrine of Apokatastasis*, 5–6.

17. Philo, *Complete Works*, under "Who is the Heir of Divine Things?" LIX. [293], Kindle location 11805.

18. A full discussion of the *apokatastasis* doctrine would include the restoration of

Another Greek word about a return or a new beginning, *palingenesia*, occurs in Matthew 19:28 in which Jesus speaks of a coming renewal of all things. His disciples, led by the questioning of Peter, are wondering what they will gain by giving up everything to follow him. Jesus tells them that at the renewal of all things (*palingenesia*) they will have an elevated position as judges over the twelve tribes of Israel. In his ministry Jesus took it for granted that a new world was coming—a new ordering of things. His invitation was to begin living the life of the coming age right now. The good news Jesus announced had to do with the current availability of God's kingdom even before God's kingdom was fully manifest in the world. Jesus taught from this point of view. As Richard Rohr notes,

> [Jesus] just assumes that things can be and will be constructed differently. Such a vision seems to be his starting point—even more than his practical goal. One has to share the "dream of God" before we know how to live and where to look for the truth. "When all is made new" in the original Greek phrase of the New Testament authors includes the word *palingenesia*—a unique word. It's rendered literally as "regeneration, a new genesis, an utterly new beginning," or, perhaps best, "a totally new birth in a totally new world." It's the only time the word is used in the Gospels. The Acts of the Apostles will use another Greek phrase, *apocatastasis*, translated in the Jerusalem Bible as "universal restoration." . . . In later theological language this term was used to describe the restoration of all creation at the end, the reconciliation of all things in Christ (see Colossians 1:20). What a hopeful and positive apocalypse that would be! I personally love to believe that is the real meaning of the victory of Christ and the final resurrection.[19]

There is a sense in the Scriptures of a coming universal restoration. And so, our fifth biblical point could be put this way: God, in Christ, has chosen to include all people in a great *apokatastasis*, a coming *palingenesia*, in which everyone will be restored so God may once again be all in all. The dream of God was not to be all in some, or some in all, but all in all. And God will persevere until this dream comes true.

---

the entire cosmos, the entire created order. This would encompass nature itself and also all other spiritual beings, including the demonic and Satan. These aspects of *apokatastasis*, especially as it relates to the devil and the demonic, have been much more controversial within the history of the church.

19. Rohr, *Jesus' Plan for a New World*, under "The New World Order" in chapter 2, Kindle location 485.

Summary

The five biblical points put forth in this chapter sketch an outline of a God who includes all in God's sovereign, saving love. This is a biblical picture of a God who is a loving parent to all, who sincerely desires to save all, who, in Christ, covers the sin of all, who is sovereign over all, and who will finally be all in all. This God is truly the Supreme Being in whom we live and move and have our being—an all-good, all-knowing, all-powerful God. Our inclusion in the ultimate plan of this God is not conditionally based on a successful spiritual transaction we make, nor is it based on our being chosen to be part of a select group of exclusive beneficiaries. The ultimate salvation of every person is solely based in God's saving grace alone, which is neither transactional nor exclusive.

Although the ultimate salvation of every person is a wonderful thought, it can still lead to deep questions. One of those questions concerns the justice and the judgment of God. How can the judgment of God fit into a scenario in which all are finally reconciled and redeemed? What about the very worst people who have ever lived? Isn't it somehow unfair if even *they* are finally saved? These are the important questions to which we turn next.

2

Judgment

> We have received a kingdom that cannot be moved–whose nature is immovable: let us have grace to serve the Consuming Fire, our God, with divine fear; not with the fear that cringes and craves, but with the bowing down of all thoughts, all delights, all loves before him who is the life of them all, and will have them all pure.
>
> —George MacDonald[1]

Love and Justice Working in Harmony

It is widely assumed, both inside and outside of Christianity, that in order to be a Christian one must believe in a God whose justice requires the permanent condemnation of many, or even most, of the people who have ever lived. It is often said in Christian circles that while God is love, God is also just, and so must finally reject all who fail to meet God's standards. This way of thinking pits the love of God and the justice of God against each other. But the love of God and the justice of God don't have to be pitted against each other. God's justice can be seen as the judging work of God which restores rather than destroys. Biblical evidence for this can be found in the following places.

---

1. MacDonald, *Unspoken Sermons*, 12.

JUDGMENT

Lamentations 3:31–33—God's Promise to Not Cast Off Forever

We begin with Lamentations 3:31–33 because here we find the Bible's clearest declaration that God's intent is *not* to cast anyone away forever. Lamentations 3:31–33 states, "For no one is cast off by the Lord forever. Although he causes grief, he will have compassion according to the abundance of his steadfast love; for he does not willingly afflict or grieve anyone." This passage from Lamentations is a profound biblical statement about the nature of God. God is not a God who rejects forever. God is a God of compassion. God is a God of abundant mercy. The full impact of this passage is even clearer when we take into account its historical context.

Lamentations comes in the Bible immediately after the book of Jeremiah, and according to tradition it was written by Jeremiah himself. It tells about a time of national catastrophe for Israel when the Jewish people were lamenting the fall of Jerusalem to the Babylonians in 587 BC. The conquering Babylonians destroyed Jerusalem and the Jerusalem temple, taking thousands of Jewish people back to Babylon as captives. How could this stunning defeat have possibly occurred? Jerusalem was God's holy city. Its walls were believed to be impossible to overcome.[2] The temple, the holy place of God on God's holy mountain, was considered by the Jewish people to be the absolute center of the world. The layout of the temple suggested that the temple itself was a microcosm of the cosmos where God dwelled and made God's presence known. Concerning how the temple functioned as a microcosm of the cosmos, Robin Parry writes,

> The temple is the cosmos writ small. When the priests and the high priest move around the temple performing their sacred duties, they are symbolically moving around the biblical cosmos. This may help explain why the temple was so central to ancient Israel and why its desecration and its destruction by pagan nations were understood as such catastrophic events. The destruction of the temple—first at the hands of Babylon and later at those of Rome—was in a very real sense, the end of the world.[3]

---

2. Lamentations 4:12 expresses the thought that Jerusalem was invincible, "The kings of the earth did not believe, nor did any of the peoples of the world, that enemies and foes could enter the gates of Jerusalem."

3. Parry, *Biblical Cosmos*, 150.

As Parry notes, the destruction of the temple raised terrifying questions in the minds of the Jewish people: Why had God allowed this destruction to happen? Was this God's final judgment on them for failing in their spiritual mission to faithfully represent God to the world? Now what? Had God rejected them forever? Was God completely done with them? Beyond being a simple lament over the fall of Jerusalem, the book of Lamentations deals with all of these questions. Lamentations is only five chapters long. It is filled with the darkness of remorse and regret. However, in the very middle of Lamentations, in chapter 3, the light breaks through. A great ray of hope pierces the clouds of regret in verses 31–33:

Verse 31: For no one is cast off by the Lord forever.

Verse 32: Though he brings grief, he will show compassion, so great is his unfailing love.

Verse 33: For he does not willingly bring affliction or grief to anyone.

These three verses in the center of Lamentations function as the mountaintop revelation of the whole book. They give voice to the highest, loftiest, most hopeful view of God in the eyes of the Jewish people. The book of Lamentations sets the kind of tone with which we should approach God: not demanding, or entitled, or swaggering, or overconfident, but humble, self-effacing, and meek. Even considering God's unfailing love, we are not in a position to order God around as if we are the ones in charge. But this doesn't mean we aren't also in a position to humbly appeal to God's character as the one who does not reject forever. This is what Jeremiah does in Lamentations, and it's an example we can follow as well.

Immediately some may wonder whether the unfailing love of God described in Lamentations is really meant for everyone or just for God's covenant people. I will argue Lamentations 3:31–33 can legitimately be read not just as a description of how God acts towards God's elect group of chosen people, but also as a declaration of how God acts towards *all* people. Robin Parry proposes reading Lamentations 3:31–33 in just this sort of way. Parry argues, "This is theology proper—an appreciation of who God is in his very being. God gets no pleasure from inflicting pain on people—his judgments are not the way he wants to relate to humanity but are his response to human sin. Punishment is an 'alien' work of God given reluctantly and after numerous warnings. In his innermost self, God is full

JUDGMENT

of loving kindness and mercy, and that is how he wants to relate to humans. Consequently, affliction is temporary and is followed by mercy."[4]

If Lamentations 3:31–33 is an accurate description of God's nature, then God's nature is best understood as unfailing love towards all—a love which does not cast off anyone forever. Though God might be compelled by love to cause grief, God derives no pleasure from it. God ultimately only causes grief as part of a long-range plan to bring God's lost children back home. The arc of God's judgment, while perhaps having to last ages upon ages, nevertheless ultimately bends back towards restoration.

There is an important detail about this passage which is lost in English translations of Lamentations 3:31. Most English translations have it that God will not reject *forever*. However, in the original Hebrew of the Old Testament, the word translated as "forever" is the Hebrew word *olam*. In the Hebrew thought world, *olam* had to do with something being far off, beyond the horizon, out of sight, but not necessarily gone forever. Taking this into account with this passage from Lamentations, this means a better understanding of this passage might go something like, "Although the Lord may, if necessary, have to grieve you and put you a long, long way out, the Lord will not take any satisfaction in causing the grief. The purpose of the grief is only to help you come back home." This difference between *forever* and *olam* is important to note, because it means rejecting someone forever is not something even being considered by God. God only considers rejecting for *olam*, not for forever. Forever rejection is not something a God of unfailing love ever even contemplates. Although God may be required to reject and cause grief for a long, long period of time, perhaps ages and ages, the duration of this rejection would only last until what is necessary has been accomplished. The rejection and the grief caused by God could very well be extremely unpleasant, even horrible. No one in their right mind would want to pursue a path in which God, out of love, is forced to make them experience rejection, penalty, and grief. Neither would anyone rationally choose to go ahead and sin, all the while knowing of a God of love who stands ready to put them through whatever grief is necessary in order to accomplish their rehabilitation.

The sobering thing about the restorative justice of a loving God is that it never relents. One might even describe this kind of restorative justice as eternal in the sense it endures forever, so long as the evil which must be conquered remains. True, we have the prerogative to store up great amounts

---

4. Parry, *Lamentations*, 106.

of evil in our hearts, but even more true is God's greater prerogative to use restorative judgments. God has all the time in the world to finally purify our hearts by making us, ever so gradually, finally able to see and feel, and even realize, that we *want* to repent from the evil we have done. In this kind of restorative judgment, we may not stay in denial forever because God will ultimately win, and our rebellious hearts will gradually be broken, restored, and set free. A loving God will never relent until everything necessary for the soul's restoration has finally come to pass. This is why all who are determined to hold on to their rebellion against God should be afraid. They should fear God, not because God will cast them off forever, but because God *won't* cast them off forever. God will never relent until the grip of sin is finally broken and they are freed from the delusions of mind which keep them from wanting to come back home. Another passage which gives great hope comes from the prophet Ezekiel, and it concerns God's promise to restore the infamous city of Sodom.

Ezekiel 16:53—The Restoration of Sodom

Another passage which powerfully speaks to the restorative purposes of God's judgments is found in Ezekiel 16:53. Here we find Ezekiel declaring God's eventual restoration of Sodom. Through Ezekiel, God makes the hopeful declaration, "I will restore the fortunes of Sodom and her daughters and of Samaria and her daughters, and [Jerusalem's] fortunes along with them." The prophet Ezekiel lived about six hundred years before the time of Christ. This prophecy comes from a time when Ezekiel was convicting Jerusalem for its sins. But Ezekiel, alongside his criticism of Jerusalem, also delivered a message of hope. Ezekiel prophesied that God would not ultimately abandon Jerusalem. Ezekiel's message to Jerusalem was, "Jerusalem, you have been really, really horrible. You've been so awful, you make even Sodom look good by comparison!"

For Ezekiel to state that Jerusalem had sunk below even Sodom was a stinging rebuke to Jerusalem's pride. The city of Sodom had set the low bar for evil in the history of the Jewish people. According to Ezekiel, God destroyed Sodom because, "She and her daughters were arrogant, overfed and unconcerned; they did not help the poor and needy. They were haughty and did detestable things before me" (Ezek 15:49–50). According to Ezekiel, God destroyed Sodom as its due punishment. The destruction of Sodom to which Ezekiel referred is found in Genesis 19, which describes how burning sulfur fell from heaven on Sodom, destroying everything, leaving only a smoking ruin. According to the New Testament in Jude 1:7, Sodom serves as an example of "those who suffer the punishment of eternal fire." Yet Ezekiel, as part of his hopeful prophecy of the eventual restoration of Jerusalem, goes on to make the stunning prophecy that God would restore the fortunes of even Sodom. It is therefore possible for God to restore even that which has been completely consumed in God's eternal judgment fire.

Here we have a perfect picture of God's restorative judgment. Sodom was thought to be the most sinful city of all. Its total destruction was carried out by burning sulfur and eternal fire. Yet God says through Ezekiel, "I will restore the fortunes of Sodom." What was there to restore? Sodom was a smoking wasteland burned with eternal fire. This helps us to see how God's eternal fire can be used for the purpose of restoration. The eternal fire of God is not a fire which necessarily burns forever, because clearly Sodom did not burn forever. The eternal fire of God is the fire of God's holy presence which finally burns away everything that is not holy. In the case of Sodom, this meant taking Sodom back to a clean slate. But this didn't mean God was done with Sodom. God's judgment of Sodom was part of God's restorative plan for the eventual restoration of Sodom.

2 Samuel 14:14—The Wise Woman of Tekoa

Second Samuel 14:14 is another passage from the Old Testament which gives us a sense of the higher restorative purposes of God's judgments. Second Samuel 14 tells the story of a woman from Tekoa who goes to King David as part of a plan to change his mind about permanently banishing David's rebellious son Absalom. In presenting her case before King David she appeals to God's character, declaring, "We must all die; we are like water spilled on the ground, which cannot be gathered up. But God will not take away a life; he will devise plans so as not to keep an outcast banished forever from his presence." Here we see the wise woman appealing to God's character. God, she argues, is not one who banishes forever, and so neither should King David be one who banishes forever. As Walter Brugemman notes, "[King] David seems to think there is virtue in keeping a grudge alive; the woman counters with the assertion that real virtue is not in keeping the banished one away but in bringing him home."[5] The wise woman sees into the heart of God and uses her insight to try to change the heart of a king.

5. Brueggemann, *First and Second Samuel*, 294.

God's purpose is not to banish God's children forever if they don't measure up. God doesn't want to banish us forever any more than any loving parent would want to banish one of their own rebellious children forever. Even in cases where God is forced to banish someone, in the larger picture, the plan is not to banish them permanently.

Matthew 5:25-26—On Having to Pay the Last Penny

When we turn to the New Testament we can also see evidence that the purpose of God's justice is not to cast off forever, but to cast off only as long as is required. In Matthew 5:25-26, we find an example of this. Here Jesus teaches, "Settle matters quickly with your adversary who is taking you to court. Do it while you are still together on the way, or your adversary may hand you over to the judge, and the judge may hand you over to the officer, and you may be thrown into prison. Truly I tell you, you will not get out until you have paid the last penny." This saying of Jesus is set within a larger context in which he is teaching on the topics of guilt and punishment. Here we get a sense of Jesus' idea of justice. For Jesus, justice meant that matters left unresolved will eventually have to be resolved before a judge. Jesus recommends resolving a situation like this before it gets to this point because, according to Jesus, if it does finally get to a judge, then the consequences will be the maximum. However, according to Jesus, even the maximum consequences of judgment will not last forever. They will fit the offense. Jesus didn't teach that the guilty parties would never get out. Jesus taught they would not get out *until they paid the last penny*. Justice, according to Jesus, did not require they never get out of jail. But justice did require, if it came to it, they not get out until they paid the last penny.

Matthew 18:21-35—The Parable of the Unforgiving Servant

In Matthew 18:21-25 we find a teaching of Jesus which contains a comparable idea about justice. This passage reads:

> Then Peter came to Jesus and asked, "Lord, how many times shall I forgive my brother or sister who sins against me? Up to seven times?" Jesus answered, "I tell you, not seven times, but seventy-seven times.
> "Therefore, the kingdom of heaven is like a king who wanted to settle accounts with his servants. As he began the settlement, a

man who owed him ten thousand bags of gold was brought to him. Since he was not able to pay, the master ordered that he and his wife and his children and all that he had be sold to repay the debt.

"At this the servant fell on his knees before him. 'Be patient with me,' he begged, 'and I will pay back everything.' The servant's master took pity on him, canceled the debt and let him go.

"But when that servant went out, he found one of his fellow servants who owed him a hundred silver coins. He grabbed him and began to choke him. 'Pay back what you owe me!' he demanded.

"His fellow servant fell to his knees and begged him, 'Be patient with me, and I will pay it back.'

"But he refused. Instead, he went off and had the man thrown into prison until he could pay the debt. When the other servants saw what had happened, they were outraged and went and told their master everything that had happened.

"Then the master called the servant in. 'You wicked servant,' he said, 'I canceled all that debt of yours because you begged me to. Shouldn't you have had mercy on your fellow servant just as I had on you?' In anger his master handed him over to the jailers to be tortured, until he should pay back all he owed.

"This is how my heavenly Father will treat each of you unless you forgive your brother or sister from your heart."

This teaching from Jesus begins with him directing his disciples to forgive not just seven times, but seventy times seven times—a number which suggests an infinitely perfect forgiveness. And then Jesus tells a parable featuring a wicked servant. This wicked servant refused to forgive a small debt owed to him right after having been forgiven an enormous debt he owed to the king. When the king found out about his wicked servant's unwillingness to forgive this small debt, the king sentenced him to be punished until he paid back all he owed the king. Notice the similarity here between the parable of the wicked servant and Jesus' teaching in Matthew 5:25–26. In Matthew 5:25–26 Jesus warns that those who end up facing the judge because they refused to settle matters quickly will be put in prison until they pay the last penny. In both instances the penalty is severe, but it eventually comes to an end. In neither case is the penalty final banishment. They are both put in prison for an extended time, but not forever. Here we can see a sense of proportionality in consequences. The lesson is that God will put us through whatever consequences are necessary. Nobody will get away with anything. We can either go the easier way or the harder way, but whichever way we will be humbled and learn our lesson. The consequences we bring on ourselves may be devastating, and may potentially last ages upon ages, but it will at last come an end.

1 Peter 3:19–20 and 4:6—Jesus' Descent to the Dead

Early Christians believed Jesus descended to the realm of the dead after his crucifixion. He descended to this realm (which they called Hades) in order proclaim the gospel to the spirits imprisoned there. They based their beliefs about Jesus' descent in the following passages found in 1 Peter:

> 1 Peter 3:19–20—After being made alive, he went and made proclamation to the imprisoned spirits—to those who were disobedient long ago when God waited patiently in the days of Noah while the ark was being built. In it only a few people, eight in all, were saved through water,

> 1 Peter 4:6—For this is the reason the gospel was preached even to those who are now dead, so that they might be judged according to human standards in regard to the body, but live according to God in regard to the spirit.

Christ's post-crucifixion descent to the dead came to be known in Christian history as his harrowing of hell. Just as Moses went to Egypt to deliver the Hebrew children from their captivity, Jesus went to Hades, the land of the dead, to deliver the dead from their captivity to death. The result of their liberation was the ability to become spiritually alive to God. This is one more reason to believe God's work with a person is not done at the end of a person's earthly life. As Heath Bradley argues,

> If Christ has conquered the power of death, as all Christians believe, then why still hold that death can keep a person from Christ? To refuse to believe that a person can come into a saving relationship with Christ in the age to come is to deny the foundational truth of the gospel that nothing, not even death, can separate us from the love of God in Christ Jesus (Romans 8:35–39). Such a refusal does not take seriously enough the victory over death that was achieved in Christ's resurrection. Because the tomb is empty, to assume that death is the deadline for grace gives death a power that it no longer has.[6]

6. Bradley, *Flames of Love*, 96.

These passages from 1 Peter help us to see that death is not the deadline for grace. Although death might be the beginning of judgment, it is not the end of grace. Grace doesn't stop when breath stops. It keeps going. It keeps working towards its ultimate goal of restoration.

William Barclay also saw great hope in the post-crucifixion descent of Christ. Barclay, in his commentary on 1 Peter 3:19–20, outlined his reasons for believing Christ continues to pursue souls past the point of death. He argued,

> There can be no salvation without repentance—but how can repentance come to those who have never been confronted with the love and holiness of God? If there is no other name by which men and women may be saved, what is to happen to those who never heard it? This is the point that the second-century Christian writer Justin Martyr fastened on to: "The Lord, the Holy God of Israel, remembered his dead, those sleeping in the earth, and came down to them to tell them the good news of salvation." The doctrine of the descent into Hades preserves the precious truth that no one who ever lived is left without a sight of Christ and without the offer of the salvation of God. Many in repeating the creed have found the phrase "He descended into hell" either meaningless or bewildering, and have quietly agreed to set it on one side and forget it. It may well be that we ought to think of this as a picture painted in terms of poetry rather than a doctrine stated in terms of theology. But it contains these three great truths—that Jesus Christ not only tasted death but drained the cup of death, that the triumph of Christ is universal and that there is no corner of the universe into which the grace of God has not reached.[7]

Barclay believed in the doctrine of second chances and was particularly encouraged in this direction as well by the phrase in 1 Peter 4:6 which speaks directly of the gospel being preached to the dead. About this passage Barclay gave the following interpretation:

> No fully satisfactory meaning has ever been found for this verse; but we think that the best explanation is as follows. For mortals, death is the penalty of sin. As Paul wrote: "Just as sin came into the world through one man, and death came through sin, and so death spread to all because all have sinned" (Romans 5:12). Had there been no sin, there would have been no death, and therefore death in itself is a judgment. So, Peter says, all people have already

---

7. Barclay, *Letters of James and Peter*, 280.

been judged when they die; in spite of that, Christ descended to the world of the dead and preached the gospel there, giving them another chance to live in the Spirit of God. In some ways, this is one of the most wonderful verses in the Bible—for, if our explanation is anywhere near the truth, it gives a breathtaking glimpse of a gospel of a second chance.[8]

As Barclay and others have noted, the two descent-to-the-dead passages from 1 Peter have inspired a wide range of scholarly debate. It's probably fair to say that these passages tend to reinforce whatever theological view one already holds. Those who believe there are no second chances after death don't find any evidence for it here. Those who believe in second and third and fourth and however-many chances find abundant evidence for it here. Yet, serious New Testament scholars find in these passages from 1 Peter a kind of ancient affirmation of the cosmic reach of Jesus' salvation. As Udo Schnell puts it, "Related to the imagery of resurrection is an exceptional piece of tradition reflected in 1 Pet. 3:19–21 and 4:6: Jesus's preaching to the spirits in prison and his preaching the gospel to the dead, which 1 Pet. 3:22 combines as Christ's 'descent into Hades' and his ascension (cf. Eph. 4:9–10). The descent to the spirits in prison makes clear that even the realms of guilt, death, and the past are not excluded from Christ's domain."[9]

Conclusion

The prophet Jeremiah said God does not cast off anyone forever (Lam 3:31). What's been shown in this chapter is that we can find agreement with this sentiment in several places in the Bible, as well as in the teaching of Jesus himself. From this we may begin to understand how the justice of God's judgment can finally work with, and not against, the love of God in the process of bringing lost children back home.

---

8. Barclay, *Letters of James and Peter*, 287.
9. Schnelle, *Theology of the New Testament*, section 11.1.2.

3

Grace

> The last word is always grace. This is the kind of
> love presupposed by evangelical universalism, and
> it is neither soft nor sentimental.
>
> —Robin Parry[1]

Three Perspectives on the Role of Grace in Salvation

WHILE ALL CHRISTIANS BELIEVE grace is necessary for salvation, all Christians have not agreed about the exact relationship between grace and salvation. One way to clarify this situation is by examining the following three propositions, each of which has been widely affirmed in the history of Christianity. Even though they are all widely affirmed, they may not be affirmed simultaneously without creating a logical conflict, and therein lies the problem. The three propositions are (1) grace alone saves, (2) grace goes to all, and (3) some will never be saved. The first proposition—grace alone saves—means grace ultimately makes salvation actual and effective, not just possible. The second proposition—grace goes to all—means God extends grace equally to all people. The third proposition—some will never be saved—means some will finally and permanently be lost to God. These three propositions—grace alone saves, grace goes to all, and some will never be saved—have all been strongly advocated in the history of Christianity, yet they can't all be affirmed without creating a logical conflict. If "grace goes to all" and "some will never be saved" are affirmed, then salvation by grace alone must be discarded. If "grace alone saves" and "some will never be saved" are affirmed, then grace going to all

---

1. MacDonald, *Evangelical Universalist*, 103.

must be discarded. And if "grace alone saves" and "grace goes to all" are affirmed, then that eliminates some never being saved. The Transactional, the Exclusive, and the Inclusive approaches (as I define them here) each solve this problem differently. How they each resolve this problem clarifies and illuminates how each understands grace.[2] We turn now to consider each of these three approaches in more detail.

1. The Transactional Solution—Reject That Grace Alone Saves

The Transactional approach affirms that grace goes to all and that some will never be saved, which forces it to reject the first proposition—grace alone saves. During the Protestant Reformation it was Jacob Arminius (1560–1609) who became the primary namesake of this approach. Arminius believed he was clarifying the meaning of the Christian faith, not creating a new kind of Christianity. He saw himself in substantial agreement with many of his contemporaries and with the teaching of the early church. Roger Olson, in his book *Arminian Theology: Myths and Realities*, explains Arminius's objective:

> Arminius did not believe he was introducing anything new to Christian theology. Whether he in fact did is debatable. He explicitly appealed to the early church fathers, used medieval theological methods and conclusions, and pointed to Protestant synergists before himself. His followers made clear that Melanchthon, an orthodox Lutheran leader, and other Lutherans held similar if not identical views. Although he did not mention the Catholic reformer Erasmus by name, it is clear that Arminius's theology was similar to his. Also the sixteenth-century Anabaptist leaders

---

2. My formulation of these three logically inconsistent propositions is inspired by a variation of a similar exercise by Thomas Talbott. Talbott's inconsistent set of three propositions are:

> (1) All human sinners are equal objects of God's redemptive love in the sense that God, being no respecter of persons, sincerely wills or desires to reconcile each one of them to himself and thus to prepare each one of them for the bliss of union with him. (2) Almighty God will triumph in the end and successfully reconcile to himself each person whose reconciliation he sincerely wills or desires. (3) Some human sinners will never be reconciled to God and will therefore remain separated from him forever. (Talbott, *Inescapable Love of God*, 38)

Balthasar Hub-maier and Menno Simons presented synergistic theologies that foreshadowed Arminius's.[3]

Arminius believed the negative effects of original sin rendered humans incapable of choosing to have faith on their own. However, grace counteracted the negative spiritual effect of original sin enough to allow each person the possibility of deciding what their eternal destiny would be. Grace lifted each person up enough for them to be able to choose to be saved if they only would. As Arminius saw it, grace did not save per se, but it did make salvation possible. For Arminius, salvation was a two-part process. God always does God's part, but if people don't do theirs, then the cooperation necessary for salvation is never realized. At some point, each person is finally on their own regarding the completion of their part of salvation.

I use the label *Arminian* as a shorthand way to describe any theology which takes a transactional approach to salvation. The Arminian approach has grown more influential since the time of the Reformation. Those who practice some form of this theology today believe no one may be saved without the assistance of grace. However, they also believe some, or many, will be eternally lost because being a recipient of grace is no absolute guarantee of salvation. This reduces grace to being God's part which makes our part possible. But, our part—however large or small—is still up to us, and grace does not assure its completion.

This often leads to spiritual insecurity for those which have some kind of Arminian theology. They can be left wondering if their faith will be counted as sufficient on judgment day. Some in this tradition take a once-saved-always-saved approach. However, if someone never seems to follow through on their faith it may be wondered if they were ever really saved in the first place. Others are quite open about the possibility of someone losing their salvation. When someone falls it's just assumed salvation has been lost for them. The Arminian approach, in its various manifestations, has had difficulty stating exactly what needs to be added to grace in order for salvation to be considered secure.

Arminian theology also has a problem regarding what is known as the age of accountability. While babies are considered innocent of unbelief, there comes a point in time when children start to become accountable. With regard to the possible consequences of this, consider the tragic example of the mentally unstable mother who became so concerned about the age of accountability and the fate of her children that she killed her

---

3. Olson, *Arminian Theology*, 22.

children before they could reach it. *The Houston Chronical* gave the following account of her reasoning:

> Andrea Pia Yates told a jail psychiatrist the day after her arrest that she drowned her five children to save them from eternal hell, the doctor testified Friday. "My children were not righteous. I let them stumble. They were doomed to perish in the fires of hell," Yates told Dr. Melissa Ferguson, the medical director of psychiatric services at the Harris County Jail. Ferguson was the first witness to testify for the defense in Yates' capital murder trial, and she painted a picture of a delusional woman obsessed with images of Satan. Ferguson said Yates told her during the first jail evaluation on June 21 that she was a bad mother. Yates cried and moaned loudly toward the end of Ferguson's assessment. "My children weren't righteous. They stumbled because I was evil," Ferguson quoted Yates as saying. "The way I was raising them they could never be saved. . . . They were going to perish."[4]

Andrea Yates was insane, but the system of religious ideas authoritatively presented to her left her with a stark conclusion for her insane mind to try and solve. She had failed as a parent. Her children were not turning out well. They were headed to hell. God would not intervene to save her children from Satan, so she would, by killing them before they reached the age of accountability. This is an extreme example of the kind of terror this theological system can incur, especially when it is attached to a doctrine of eternal torment. Boyd Purcell, in his book *Spiritual Terrorism*, makes the following observation about Sally Yates: "Thoughts came into her head that she needed to do the best thing for her children, before they were corrupted by the evil world, and kill them so they could go on to heaven. I know that this sounds crazy because it is crazy, but, based on her crazy religious brainwashing, in context, it makes sense. She apparently, reasoned thusly: Why would any loving parents stand by and let their children almost certainly go to hell, to be tortured forever, when they could send them on to heaven?"[5] As Purcell points out, there is a very dark logic which can develop in the Arminian theological system.

Arminian theology also raises questions because it simultaneously affirms God's desire for everyone to be saved, while also asserting that it will never happen. What is the explanation? Why is God not able to do

---

4. Christian and Teachey, "Yates Believed Children Doomed."
5. Purcell, *Spiritual Terrorism*, 77–78.

something God expressly wants to do? Why is God defeated in God's own will to save all? Isn't God the one no one is able to withstand (2 Chron 20:6)? Is not God able to do whatever God pleases (Ps 115:3)? Isn't it the purpose of God, rather than the plans of human minds, that will be established (Prov 19:21)? Isn't it the case that no purpose of God may be thwarted (Job 42:2; Isa 14:24)? Isn't God the one who declares the end from the beginning (Isa 46:10)? Isn't God the one for whom nothing is too hard and for whom all things are possible (Jer 32:27; Matt 19:26)? Isn't God the one who works everything in conformity with the purpose of his will (Eph 1:11)? Transactional approaches, like that of Arminian theology, have to find a way to explain how God, on the one hand, can want all people to be saved, yet, on the other hand, know from the beginning about people who will come to inevitably tragic endings.

To be fair, the Transactional/Arminian approach doesn't see itself as proclaiming a weak God as much as it sees itself as having a strong view of human self-determination when it comes to spiritual destinies. It gives people a sense of control and accomplishment. It puts people in the driver's seat when it comes to salvation. Anybody can be saved, if they will only do what needs to be done. If people end up being lost to God forever, it's not God's fault. It's their fault. Along these lines, British scholar N. T. Wright argues that people, by their own choices, have the ability to walk down a road which leads to their own destruction. He describes their journey to doom as follows:

> My suggestion is that it is possible for human beings so to continue down this [evil] road, so to refuse all whisperings of good news, all glimmers of the true light, all promptings to turn and go the other way, all signposts to the love of God, that after death they become at last, by their own effective choice, beings that once were human but now are not, creatures that have ceased to bear the divine image at all. With the death of that body in which they inhabited God's good world, in which the flickering flame of goodness had not been completely snuffed out, they pass simultaneously not only beyond hope but also beyond pity. There is no concentration camp in the beautiful countryside, no torture chamber in the palace of delight. Those creatures that still exist in an ex-human state, no longer reflecting their maker in any meaningful sense, can no longer excite in themselves or others the natural sympathy some feel even for the hardened criminal.[6]

---

6. Wright, *Surprised by Hope*, 182–83.

N. T. Wright is a good example of how many who take a Transactional approach solve the problem of a God who wants to save all but may not able to do so. God's judgment for noncompliant souls is simply to allow them to devolve past the point of meaningful existence. It's not that God sends them away. They send themselves away, and God doesn't stop them. In so doing they devolve into ex-human creatures for whom nobody, including their parents, can even feel sorrow. Approaches like this suggest that while God doesn't actively throw people away forever, God does allow people to throw themselves away forever.

Others who take a Transactional approach insist God most definitely *does* cast people away forever. For example, Franklin Graham argues God actively casts those who are spiritually wanting into a hell of no return. In an interview with Bill O'Reilly, Graham put it this way, "The Bible is very clear. There is a hell. And if you look at Revelation chapter 20, not only is a person condemned to hell, they are *thrown* into hell. That's how serious it is."[7]

Whether it's God who does the casting, or people who do it to themselves, the Transactional approach gives up the proposition that grace alone saves. Grace, although it goes to all, doesn't accomplish all of salvation for anyone. Especially for churches in the Protestant tradition, the rejection of salvation by grace alone is a dramatic move. Salvation by grace alone, *sola gratis* in the Latin, was one of the great rallying cries of the Protestant Reformation. Yet in the Transactional approach salvation is not by grace alone. Anyone who is finally saved is only saved because they were able to add something to grace that grace did not guarantee. Grace alone wasn't enough. Something had to be added to it. No matter how small that addition to grace was, it remains true that without that addition the person ends up doomed for eternity. And the rejection of salvation by grace alone isn't even the greatest difficulty the Transactional approach faces, because it also raises even more serious questions about the goodness of God.

If we accept that God knows the end from the beginning, as is stated in Isaiah 46:10, then God knows in advance about those who will be given grace yet still not be saved. Nevertheless, God allows these ill-fated people to come into existence and then to proceed inevitably towards their ultimate doom. Even though they are given the chance to make their own choices, they still exist in a creation in which their spiritual failure is foreknown and inescapable. This poses a substantial threat to the perfect goodness of God.

---

7. Graham in an interview with Bill O'Reilly on *The O'Reilly Factor*: Samaritans Purse, "Franklin Graham - O'Reilly Factor."

How can God be all-good and yet condemn people whom God knows in advance will fail? How can God be perfectly good yet set into motion a creation which produces personal destinies of certain disaster? These bad outcomes ultimately rebound back to God. As David Bentley Hart phrases it, "One way or another, after all, all causes are logically reducible to their first cause. This is no more than a logical truism. And it does not matter whether one construes the relation between primary and secondary causality as one of total determinism or as one of utter indeterminacy, for in either case all 'consequents' are—either as actualities or merely as possibilities—contingent upon their primordial 'antecedent,' apart from which they could not exist."[8] In other words, it matters not whether God causes bad outcomes directly or indirectly, God still knowingly causes them one way or another, and that causes a problem for the Transactional approach with regard to God's perfect goodness.

While the problem of God condemning people who effectively have no chance at being saved is not so obvious in the Transactional approach, it is extremely obvious in the Exclusive approach. Although the Exclusive approach affirms that salvation is by grace alone, it does not affirm that God extends this kind of saving grace to all. That means some will never be saved because they were never given the saving grace in the first place. It's to this approach that we turn next.

2. The Exclusive Solution—
Reject That Grace Goes to All

The Exclusive approach affirms proposition (1) grace alone saves, and proposition (3) some will never be saved, forcing it to reject proposition (2) grace goes to all. This approach to Christian theology has a long history which can be traced back to the early centuries of the church. St. Augustine (354–430) is often credited for initiating it. During the Protestant Reformation, John Calvin (1509–1564) crystalized this approach in a theological system which incorporated many of Augustine's thoughts. According to Calvin, God's grace saves everyone to whom God gives it. Calvin believed grace is, by definition, saving. Grace was the *certain* saving presence of God in the life of fallen individuals. Grace was what caused them to have faith, and to believe, and to grow, and to persevere in the faith. However, Calvin also believed this kind of saving grace was exclusively for those whom God

---

8. Hart, *That All Shall Be Saved*, 70.

had elected for salvation. Over time Calvin's theological approach was developed by others into a theological tradition called Calvinism. I use the labels *Calvinism* or *Calvinist* as a shorthand way to describe what I call the Exclusive approach to Christian theology. I call it Exclusive because it excludes all but the elect from the possibility of salvation.

What makes the exclusion of the non-elect so troubling is that they are excluded not because of anything they did, or anything they would have done. God does not look into the future to see who will be deserving and then on the basis of that condition select them to receive saving grace. All humans are understood to be undeserving because of the fallen and rebellious state of original sin into which they are born. They all inherit their status as spiritual rebels and will deny God to the end without the intervention of grace. God, according to the mysteries of God's will, decides to save some by giving them the grace of God's saving, faith-inducing presence in their lives. Christ's sacrificial death on the cross, even though powerful enough to save all, is understood to be limited to the particular purpose of saving the elect. God, as they reason it, never intended to save everyone.

Calvinists actually make a distinction regarding grace. They recognize a Common Grace, which goes to all, and a Special Grace, which goes only to the elect. Common grace is made up of the general blessings of life from which all people benefit, but it does not lead to salvation. Special Grace, however, always results in faith and salvation for those who are elected to receive it. Those who only receive Common Grace are never saved. Those who receive Common Grace *and* Special Grace are always saved.

This is all seen as good news because, as Calvinists see it, God would be quite justified in condemning us all. Further, the magnitude of salvation by grace alone will be made all the more precious to the elect as they contemplate the damned souls they consider to be justly condemned to hell for all eternity. Calvinists understand their system of belief not as the doctrines of an unfair God, but as the doctrines of grace. Calvinists have a strong view of the sovereignty of God. Their God is a God who is in charge of—sovereign over—all human destinies. This God is powerful enough to save all who are elected for salvation. Grace does not just give the elect hope of salvation. Grace gives the elect the certainty of salvation.

A quick way to summarize Calvinist thought according to its most distinctive elements is through the acronym TULIP. The T stands for total depravity, which refers to the fallen state of will and mind into which all humans are born due to original sin. This depravity negatively affects their spiritual ability, rendering them powerless to generate faith on their own. Faith only appears in the life of the elect because God chooses to overcome the effects of total depravity and generate faith in them. The U stands for unconditional election, meaning God does not elect people on the condition of knowing they will one day believe. God knows, because of Adam and Eve's original sin being passed down to all humanity, that no totally depraved human being will ever believe without God's intervention. God chooses the elect solely on the basis of God's own desire. They become included in the exclusive group of the elect but not because of any spiritual transaction they successfully complete with God. In this sense their inclusion is non-transactional. They don't do anything to deserve it. The L stands for limited atonement, in that the purpose of the atonement, even though it was powerful enough to save all people, was limited in effect for the particular purpose of saving the elect. The I stands for irresistible grace, meaning that once God opens their hearts, the elect will not fail to respond to the gospel. In other words, the gracious calling of God is always effective in those whom God elects to be delivered from their spiritual depravity. The P stands for the perseverance of the saints, meaning that because of God's continual superintending, all of the elect will be found to be persevering in the faith at the time of their death. God will not fail to successfully shepherd home all of the elect.

This summary of Calvinism through the five points of the TULIP acronym captures its distinctive clarity. However, Calvinism's clarity still often results in a lack of clarity among its practitioners about who will actually be saved in the end. Due to their understanding of the doctrine of the perseverance of the saints, if someone falls away and then dies outside the faith, that means they were never elect in the first place. Therefore, in Calvinism there can often be life-long uncertainty about whether or not one is actually among the elect, for the elect only know if they are elect if at the judgment they are found by God to have truly persevered in the faith. This results in much intense discipleship in Calvinist churches, but practically it doesn't give Calvinists much assurance of salvation along the way. The early church father Augustine, whom many Calvinists look upon as a kind of patron saint, did not see any final spiritual security for Christians in this life. In his treatise entitled *On Predestination and the Perseverance of the Saints*, Augustine stated, "I assert, therefore, that the perseverance by which we persevere in Christ even to the end is the gift of God . . . Therefore, it is uncertain whether *anyone* has received this gift so long as he is still alive."[9]

---

9. Augustine, *On Predestination*, under Chapter 1, "Of the Nature of the Perseverance

By extension, Calvinist parents, even though they may become convinced they themselves are among the elect, can't know what the fate of their children will be. Robin Parry quotes the prominent Calvinist minister John Piper along these lines. Piper once said of his own children:

> I have three sons. Every night after they are asleep I turn on the hall light, open their bedroom door, and walk from bed to bed, laying my hands on them and praying. Often I am moved to tears of joy and longing. I pray that Karsten Luke become a great physician of the soul, that Benjamin John become the beloved son of my right hand in the gospel, and that Abraham Christian give glory to God as he grows strong in his faith. But I am not ignorant that God may not have chosen my sons for his sons. And, though I think I would give my life for their salvation, if they should be lost to me, I would not rail against the Almighty. He is God. I am but a man. The potter has absolute rights over the clay. Mine is to bow before his unimpeachable character and believe that the Judge of all the earth has ever and always will do right.[10]

Notice how Piper seems certain he is one of the elect. Since he had obviously not yet died while persevering in the faith at the time he expressed these thoughts, I don't know how he could have been absolutely sure of this. Nevertheless, his concern for his children arises from the fact that according to his Calvinist approach to theology it may be God's will to eternally torment all three of them. As Piper sees it, there is no guarantee that any of his children are among the elect of God.

Calvinism teaches that some never even have a chance for salvation. According to Calvinism, if people are not elect, they have absolutely no chance at all of ever being saved. They are born with no hope of salvation. They die with no hope of salvation. They end up being damned to hell forever even though they never had a chance. This poses a significant challenge to the goodness of God, and it leads to the charge that the God of Calvinism is mean, or cruel, or perhaps even evil. This is especially true when this approach is paired with the doctrine of eternal conscious torment. How can God still be good if God brings non-elect souls into existence without their consent, and then eternally torments them for failing to have faith, even though they never had any hope of generating faith on their own?

Here Discoursed Of," Kindle location 823. Emphasis Mine.

10. MacDonald, *Evangelical Universalist*, 243.

Calvinism, since it asserts that God does not sincerely desire for all people to be saved, also must deal with the Scriptures which suggest that God does desire the salvation of each person. After all, did not God intend to bless all the peoples of the earth through Abraham (Gen 12:3)? Was it not God's purpose to draw all people through Christ (John 12:32)? Does not God, like a shepherd, desire to save all the lost sheep (Luke 15: 4–7)? Is not God our Savior, who desires everyone to be saved and to come to the knowledge of the truth (1 Tim 2:3–4)? Is not God the one who is patient with us, not wanting anyone to perish, but everyone to come to repentance (2 Pet 3:9)? Those who take a Calvinistic approach must explain why it is that God does not desire to save all who are in need of salvation.

Here we should pause to note a technical nuance in Calvinism which allows Calvinists to assert that God actually does will the salvation of all, but that God's will to save all is superseded by God's will to magnify God's glory. John Piper explains it this way: "God's will for all people to be saved is not at odds with the sovereignty of his grace in election, with all the achievements of his grace that flow from that election. . . . What restrains God's will to save all people is his supreme commitment to uphold and display the full range of his glory. His plan from all eternity was to magnify his glory in creation and redemption. He aimed to make the glory of his grace the highest revelation of himself (Eph. 1:6)."[11] Although there is a certain logic about how God's highest will with regard to glory supersedes God's lower will to save all people, it doesn't provide much comfort for those not being saved. In the end, effectively, God still is more committed to displaying glory than to saving all of God's children, which one might argue would be a better way for God to magnify God's glory.

Even considering all of these challenges, the Calvinist approach commands a strong following. There are biblical passages which may be used to support its core arguments. It teaches the sovereignty of God over human affairs. It places salvation squarely in the hands of God. It offers a grace which is 100 percent effective in saving all those to whom this grace is given. It understands God to be continually and forever at the side of all of the elect, not losing a single one.

Calvinism, as a Protestant theology, was extremely influential in colonial America, especially among the Puritans. Jonathan Edwards, considered one of the greatest, if not the greatest, early American theologian, was a Calvinist. Although Calvinism is not as prominent today as it once was,

---

11. Piper, *Does God Desire All to Be Saved?*, 54.

it is still a very influential theology, especially among Evangelicals. And it appears to be on the rise. *The New York Times* noted this in an article appearing January 3, 2014:

> If you have joined a church that preaches a Tulip theology, does that mean a) the pastor bakes flowers into the communion wafers, b) the pastor believes that flowers that rise again every spring symbolize the resurrection, or c) the pastor is a Calvinist? As an increasing number of Christians know, the answer is "c." The acronym summarizes John Calvin's so-called doctrines of grace, with their emphasis on sinfulness and predestination. The T is for man's Total Depravity. The U is for Unconditional Election, which means that God has already decided who will be saved, without regard to any condition in them, or anything they can do to earn their salvation. The acronym gets no cheerier from there. Evangelicalism is in the midst of a Calvinist revival. Increasing numbers of preachers and professors teach the views of the 16th-century French reformer. Mark Driscoll, John Piper and Tim Keller—megachurch preachers and important evangelical authors—are all Calvinist. Attendance at Calvin-influenced worship conferences and churches is up, particularly among worshipers in their 20s and 30s.
>
> In the Southern Baptist Convention, the country's largest Protestant denomination, the rise of Calvinism has provoked discord. In a 2012 poll of 1,066 Southern Baptist pastors conducted by LifeWay Research, a nonprofit group associated with the Southern Baptist Convention, 30 percent considered their churches Calvinist—while twice as many were concerned "about the impact of Calvinism."[12]

The impact of the Exclusive approach in Calvinism is still being felt today. This tradition affirms proposition (1) grace alone saves, and proposition (3) some will never be saved. They will never be saved because they were never elected for salvation in the first place. It gives up proposition (2) grace goes to all. The Exclusive approach agrees with the Inclusive approach that grace alone saves, and it agrees with the Transactional approach that all will not be saved. Only the Inclusive approach argues that all will be saved, and it is to this approach we now turn.

---

12. Oppenheimer, "Calvinist Revival."

3. The Inclusive Solution—
Reject That Some Will Never Be Saved

The Inclusive approach to Christian theology maintains proposition (1) grace alone saves, and proposition (2) grace goes to all. This forces it to reject proposition (3) some will never be saved. Because this approach affirms that everyone is included in salvation it is sometimes just called universalism, and this can cause confusion because universalism is such a generic term. The Inclusive approach described here is more accurately called Christian universalism because it seeks to be distinctively Christian. Christian universalism is a self-consciously Christian approach to theology which is rooted in Scripture and which was widely present in the early centuries of the church. It affirms the absolute centrality of Jesus as the only path for the ultimate redemption of humanity. It is not a pluralistic approach which suggests all spiritual paths are equal. When I use the term Christian universalism I am using it to describe God's universal parental love for all people, God's universal desire for all to be saved, God's universal covering of humanity's sin in Christ, God's universal sovereignty over human destiny, and God's universal intent to finally be all in all. While this theology may fairly be called a universal kind of Christianity, it is not a Christless pluralism which does away with his centrality in human salvation. Robin Parry, in his book *The Evangelical Universalist,* used an imaginary person named Anastasia to describe this type of Christian approach:

> I wish to introduce you to an imaginary representative of Christian universalism. We shall call her Anastasia. She will represent a version of Christian universalism I consider to have plausible grounds for claiming to be a position in tune with Scripture. Let me sketch her views. Anastasia is an evangelical Christian. She believes in the inspiration and authority of the Bible. She believes in all those crucial Christian doctrines such as Trinity, creation, sin, atonement, the return of Christ, salvation through Christ alone, by grace alone, through faith alone. In fact, on most things you'd be hard pressed to tell her apart from any other evangelical. Contrary to what we may suspect, she even believes in the eschatological wrath of God—in hell. She differs most obviously in two unusual beliefs. First, she believes that one's eternal destiny is not fixed at death and, consequently, that those in hell can repent and throw themselves upon the mercy of God in Christ and thus be saved. Second, she also believes that in the end everyone will do this. Now, not all Christian universalists would agree with Anastasia's

views here, but it is her kind of universalism that I primarily have in mind when I speak of universalism.[13]

The Inclusive/Christian universalist approach agrees with the Exclusive/Calvinist approach in certain key areas: that salvation is by grace alone, and that God is completely sovereign over human destiny. It also agrees with the Transactional/Arminian approach in certain key areas: that God gives grace to all people, and that God wants all people to be saved. Because Christian universalists believe grace alone saves and everyone gets grace, they must therefore give up on proposition (3) some will never be saved.

One of the strengths of this approach is how it allows for the necessary assurance needed for healthy spiritual growth. Without the assurance that God really has us, we might always carry with us a burden of morbid fear. Unless we can believe God is with us not just *if* we get things right, but *until* we get things right, then our spirituality could be driven by an unhealthy fear of rejection. In the Transactional/Arminian approach we could be left wondering whether or not we've added enough to grace in order to pass muster on judgment day. In the Exclusive/Calvinist approach we could be left wondering if we were ever really included among the elect in the first place. Only in the Inclusive/Christian universalist approach do we experience the full safety and ultimate confidence which true love provides.

Christian universalists believe God's decision for us is so decisive it will ultimately overcome everything working against us, including our own deluded decisions along the way. However, some may ask, "If we've all been eternally included, and if we'll all eventually experience full reconciliation with God, then what motivation is there to follow Christ and to grow spiritually right now?" One answer is because sin is anti-life and anti-love. Sin brings misery not only to ourselves, but also to others. Even though God's necessary, love-driven judgments on sin may not lead to never-ending death or never-ending torment, the consequences of sin are still extremely serious and may last a very, very, very long time. Those who are determined to resist, like the prodigal son, will eventually tire of the consequences of sin. In a God-driven moment of inspiration they will finally come to their senses. After they are restored to their right minds, they will want nothing more than to begin their journey home. Once they have discovered their true will, they will be ready and willing to work through whatever consequences their sins have brought upon themselves, and they will sincerely wish they had never wandered off the good path in the first place.

13. MacDonald, *Evangelical Universalist*, 6.

However, the main reason to grow spiritually is not to avoid judgment, but to begin journeying right now into everything which is good about experiencing God's kingdom in the present moment. The good news which Jesus announced hinged on his declaration that the kingdom of God is at hand (Mark 1:14). The sooner we awake in faith to all the good things of God, the better off we are right now. This approach to spiritual growth is about the joyful prospect of entering more and more fully into the eternal life of the perfectly good God—the God who has, through Christ, already eternally accepted and included each of us by grace. It's about wanting to experience what Jesus said he had come to give us—not just life, but life to the full (John 10:10).

If we take this approach, however, we will have to rethink what hell has commonly been understood to mean. It will also mean understanding that the road of grace will take us through as much hell—both in this life and the next—as it takes in order for us to come to our senses. Being put back right can't come without faith in Christ, because there is no putting things back right without Christ and his perfect sacrifice on our behalf. We don't earn our salvation through our punishment. We are not saved by our punishment. We are saved by Christ. But as part of that process there may be some hell to pay. The goodness of God does not exempt us from the consequences of our actions—quite the opposite. The goodness of God compels God to put us through whatever corrective measures become necessary. To put it bluntly, we *can* have as much hell as we want, and we *will* have as much hell as we need. That's a sobering thought. And it's to this bracing thought which we turn next.

4

Hell

> Hell exists, so long as it exists, only as the last terrible residue of a fallen creation's enmity to God, the lingering effects of a condition of slavery that God has conquered universally in Christ and will ultimately conquer individually in every soul.
>
> —David Bentley Hart[1]

Hell as a Place of Restoration

TAKING THE INCLUSIVE/CHRISTIAN UNIVERSALIST approach means rethinking what hell has commonly been understood to mean. In this approach, hell is not a place of permanent separation from God, but a place of restorative justice where a person feels the full corrective presence of God. Some take any reference to hell in the Bible to mean a place of either eventual annihilation or never-ending torment. However, by looking at the cultural context and the original languages in which the Bible was written, one can see room for a different understanding. The following passages each mention hell, or a place of punishment. But, as I will argue, there is room to see that this punishment does not necessarily result in eternal exclusion. We begin with Matthew 5:21–30.

Matthew 5:21–30—On Being in Danger of the Fire of Hell

The fifth chapter of Matthew contains an extended teaching about judgment. In Matthew 5:21–30 we read:

---

1. Hart, *That All Shall Be Saved*, 81.

"You have heard that it was said to the people long ago, 'You shall not murder, and anyone who murders will be subject to judgment.' But I tell you that anyone who is angry with a brother or sister will be subject to judgment. Again, anyone who says to a brother or sister, 'Raca,' is answerable to the court. And anyone who says, 'You fool!' will be in danger of the fire of hell.

"Therefore, if you are offering your gift at the altar and there remember that your brother or sister has something against you, leave your gift there in front of the altar. First go and be reconciled to them; then come and offer your gift.

"Settle matters quickly with your adversary who is taking you to court. Do it while you are still together on the way, or your adversary may hand you over to the judge, and the judge may hand you over to the officer, and you may be thrown into prison. Truly I tell you, you will not get out until you have paid the last penny.

"You have heard that it was said, 'You shall not commit adultery.' But I tell you that anyone who looks at a woman lustfully has already committed adultery with her in his heart. If your right eye causes you to stumble, gouge it out and throw it away. It is better for you to lose one part of your body than for your whole body to be thrown into hell. And if your right hand causes you to stumble, cut it off and throw it away. It is better for you to lose one part of your body than for your whole body to go into hell."

The context of Jesus' teaching here concerned relationships between people. Jesus warned how even thinking evil thoughts towards others makes one guilty and in danger of facing judgment. Jesus gave two specific examples of behaviors which lead to guilt: angry name-calling and lustful looking. Jesus condemned both of these actions in the strongest terms possible within Jewish culture. In this passage Jesus refers to the danger of the fire of hell, literally about the danger of condemnation in a place called *Gehenna* in the original Greek text of the New Testament.[2] Jesus also warned that justice will always eventually be served, noting that unresolved matters reaching a judge will result in the judge pronouncing a sentence which will not be reduced. The sentence would be served, according to Jesus, "until you have paid the last penny." Notice that the sentence is not the death penalty or a life sentence. The sentence eventually comes to an end when "the last penny is paid." With thoughts of Gehenna

---

2. Jesus references Gehenna in the following passages: Matt 5:22; 5:29; 5:30; 10:28; 18:9; 23:15; 23:33; Mark 9:43; 9:45; 9:47; Luke 12:5.

and of strict judges requiring payment down to the last penny, we can turn more generally to Jesus' warnings about hell.

Hell and Biblical Translation

The word "hell" did not exist in the time of Jesus. "Hell" is an English word which gradually came to be associated with anything happening "down there" in the "bad place." When the Bible was first translated into English, the word "hell" was often used in both the Old and New Testaments to translate a variety of Hebrew and Greek words, none of which meant the never-ending, fiery torture pit that hell came to represent in medieval times. The use of the single word "hell" to translate a variety of different Greek and Hebrew terms having to do with judgment led to misunderstandings. For instance, in the Old Testament there is not really a developed idea of an afterlife. Ancient Jews thought that after death everyone descended to the shadowy realm of the dead they called *Sheol*. However, the King James Version, completed in 1611, often translated "Sheol" as "hell," leaving the appearance that hell was equally present in the Old Testament and the New Testament. To the first readers of the Bible in English it seemed hell was a permanent fixture of the Bible which had been present from the beginning. Thankfully, modern translations of the Bible have refrained from using the word "hell" as a simple substitute for "Sheol." As a result, there is less and less hell in modern Bible translations.

The original Greek language of the New Testament records Jesus using the words "Hades" and "Gehenna" in reference to places of judgment. The King James Bible translated both these words with the English word "hell," thereby obscuring their different meanings. First, let's look at Hades. "Hades," a word with a Greek background, was a general equivalent of the Hebrew concept of Sheol, the general abode of the dead. Brad Jersak, in his book *Her Gates Will Never Be Shut*, gives the following concise overview of Sheol's place in the Bible:

> In the Old Testament, Sheol (Hades in the Septuagint, the Greek translation of the Hebrew Bible) can refer to death or the grave where everyone goes—righteous or wicked (Psalm 16:10), but the faithful hope to be rescued from it (Psalm 16:10). Sometimes it is under the earth (Isaiah 7:11; 57:9; Ezekiel 31:14; Psalm 86:13), under the mountains (Job 26:5), under water (Jonah 2:7), or far from heaven (Job 11:8; Amos 9:2; Psalm 139:8). It is monotonous

and gloomy (Job 3:17–19), a place of sorrows (Psalm 18:5), a place for the wicked (Psalm 9:17; Isaiah 14:9–19), parallel to destruction (Proverbs 15:11), or a place of torment (Luke 16:23). It can be a pit, an abyss, or a prison (Ezekiel 31:16–17). . . .

In the New Testament, Hades may still refer to either death or the place where the dead are confined until Judgment Day (Revelation 20:13). It can be a place of conscious torment opposite to paradise or the "bosom of Abraham" (Luke 16:22–23), a fate reserved for the unregenerate (Matthew 11:23; Luke 10:15). Hades also represents the forces of darkness that oppose the Church (Matthew 16:18). Hades is finally exterminated in the lake of fire (Revelation 6:8; 20:14).[3]

As Jersak notes, neither Sheol nor Hades were understood to be places of eternal torment in the time of Jesus. The non-eternalness of Hades is underscored by the book of Revelation's description of Hades itself being thrown into the Lake of Fire (Rev 20:14).

Having looked at Hades, now let's consider Gehenna. Most grant that Hades didn't have to do with eternal torment. But when it comes to Jesus' references to Gehenna in certain judgment passages, this is when it's argued that Jesus was referring to a place of unending torment in flames. "Gehenna," a word with a Hebrew background, literally means "the Valley of Hinnom." Gehenna was a valley just south of Jerusalem which had developed a terrible reputation. In Gehenna, in the days before Jesus, desperate Jews gave up on their faith and made fiery human sacrifices of their children in the worship of other gods. The Israelite king Josiah had the valley formally desecrated by the scattering of ashes so it could not any further be used as a place to worship these foreign deities. Not long afterwards, the Hebrew prophet Jeremiah held Gehenna up as a valley of destruction where one day the bodies of the inhabitants of Jerusalem herself would be disposed of after being defeated in battle.[4] When Jesus used the term "Gehenna" in

---

3. Jersak, *Gates Will Never Be Shut*, 18.

4. Jeremiah's prophecy as found in Jeremiah 19:6–9, """So beware, the days are coming, declares the Lord, when people will no longer call this place Topheth or the Valley of Ben Hinnom, but the Valley of Slaughter.

""'In this place I will ruin the plans of Judah and Jerusalem. I will make them fall by the sword before their enemies, at the hands of those who want to kill them, and I will give their carcasses as food to the birds and the wild animals. I will devastate this city and make it an object of horror and scorn; all who pass by will be appalled and will scoff because of all its wounds. I will make them eat the flesh of their sons and daughters, and they will eat one another's flesh because their enemies will press the siege so hard against them to destroy them.'"""

his warning, all of this background would have come into the minds of his hearers. They would have thought of Gehenna as the hideous place where bodies come to ruin and destruction, not as a place of eternal torment. The morphing of Gehenna into a place of eternal torment did not begin to occur until after the time of Jesus.[5]

When we are trying to understand the warnings of Jesus, we need to keep in mind what Jesus was doing. Jesus was warning his contemporaries of the desperate and destructive consequences of sin in the most vivid metaphoric imagery his Jewish contemporaries knew about. When Jesus used the term "Gehenna," this brought to their minds a smoldering, terrible, festering place of dishonor and ruin. To the Jewish mind, ending up having one's carcass left to be consumed in Gehenna was the worst fate imaginable. And when Jesus was warning about all of this, he wasn't just talking about something each individual Jewish person needed to think about. Jesus was also warning about the fate of the entire Jewish nation of his day.

The Larger Context of Jesus' Warnings

What I first failed to understand about Jesus' warnings was how they were connected to his sense of an impending national disaster for Israel. Jesus warned of a looming disaster which would befall Jerusalem within a generation of those to whom he was preaching. This disaster, this tribulation, would result in the destruction of both Jerusalem and the temple. Jesus predicted this coming disaster would be a "great distress, unequaled from the beginning of the world until now—and never to be equaled again" (Matt 24:21). Jesus advised the people of his day not to get caught up in the leadership of what he called the corrupt generation which was leading Israel into a violent conflict with Rome. He warned his followers not to go into Jerusalem when the Roman armies came, but rather to head for the hills (Luke 21:21).

What Jesus predicted actually came to pass. Jesus' crucifixion and resurrection took place in AD 33. In AD 70 Jerusalem was destroyed and the temple was burned. Jerusalem, with its high walls and spiritual significance, was considered a safe haven. Therefore, many Jews from outlying areas sought refuge in Jerusalem as the Roman armies advanced upon

---

5. Kim Papaioannou argues this point well in *The Geography of Hell in the Teaching of Jesus*. Papaioannou shows that there was no fixed meaning of "Gehenna" at the time of Jesus. He also argues persuasively that the connection between Gehenna and eternal torment is not evident until after the time of Jesus.

them. By the time the Roman siege of Jerusalem was complete, there were so many dead bodies to be disposed of that they ended up piling them in Gehenna, in the Valley of Hinnom. The Roman historian Josephus described the destruction of Jerusalem in AD 70. The trapped occupants of Jerusalem tried to go over the walls of the city, which meant facing the Roman army on the ramparts they had built around the city walls. When the desperate residents of the city came over the walls, the Romans crucified them. But there were so many dying in the city that there was nothing to do with the bodies. Josephus described how the people in Jerusalem handled the problem of the rising count of the dead. Brad Jersak quotes Josephus regarding their terrible solution:

> Now the seditious at first gave orders that the dead should be buried out of the public treasury, as not enduring the stench of their dead bodies. But afterwards, when they could not do that, they had them cast down from the walls into the valleys beneath [i.e., Gehenna and Kidron]. However, when Titus, in going his rounds along those valleys, saw them full of dead bodies, and the thick putrefaction running about them, he gave a groan; and, spreading out his hands to heaven, called God to witness that this was not his doing; and such was the sad case of the city itself.[6]

Josephus, himself Jewish by descent, chronicled the destruction of Jerusalem for the Romans. As Jersak points out, Josephus's grisly account of this disaster shows how the valley of Gehenna became itself a burial ground for those who followed along with the violent and corrupt generation Jesus warned about. Paul Ellis gives the following chilling summary of the fall of Jerusalem:

> The fall of Jerusalem in AD70 was unprecedented in horror and magnitude. By first-century standards, the number of deaths was simply mind-boggling. In a city that was home to around 200,000, more than a million people died. Allowing Passover pilgrims into the city was a dirty trick [by the Romans] because it added pressure to already-limited food supplies. (The tyrants had burned the grain stores just a few weeks earlier.) The resulting famine brought unspeakable misery to those trapped inside . . . More than 600,000 bodies were thrown out of the city gates, and the lanes were filled with bodies . . . In desperation, people ate everything . . . Starvation drove many Jews over the wall, but those caught by the Romans were crucified atop their embankment.

6. Jersak, *Gates Will Never Be Shut*, 60. Bracketed addition by Jersak.

This horrific act was meant to frighten the defenders into surrender. It didn't work. The starving continued to flee because they esteemed death from their enemies, even a brutal death by crucifixion, to be preferable to the slow death of starvation. At one point the Romans were crucifying as many as 500 people per day. There were so many crucifixions that the Romans ran out of wood. Jesus said, "There will be great and unprecedented distress" and there was. The siege of Jerusalem was genocide on an industrial scale, a first-century holocaust. In words reminiscent of Christ's prophecy, Josephus said the siege of Jerusalem exceeded all "the misfortunes of men from the beginning of the world."[7]

If we imagine Jesus clearly seeing all of this destruction and disaster coming towards Jerusalem then his many warnings to his own generation make much more sense. All of this gruesome background is important because when we talk about Jesus and "hell" we need to have in the back of our minds that when Jesus talked about "hell" he used the word "Gehenna." "Gehenna," at the time of Jesus, was not an abstract word which only referred to an otherworldly place of judgment. Gehenna, in Jesus' day, was a real-world place which symbolized judgment, death, and destruction, but not necessarily a place of unending torment. As things turned out, within a generation of Jesus' warnings, Gehenna, the Valley of Hinnom, was literally filled with the bodies of thousands upon thousands of Jews killed by Rome. When Jesus warned his fellow Jews about ending up in Gehenna, that was an actual place they knew all about. Gehenna represented destruction. For a Jew of that time there was no more terrible fate to be imagined than having one's body tossed into Gehenna to be destroyed. In the Jewish mind Gehenna was the place of ultimate disgrace, and so when Jesus wanted to really get the attention of his fellow Jews regarding judgment, that was the term he used.

When I think of Jesus' mission to the Jewish nation of his day I see a man warning a whole nation and the leaders of that nation. Jesus was warning them saying, "You are on the road to Gehenna. All of your traditions have blinded you to what's really going on. You have lost your way. You are violent and corrupt and you don't even know it. You are blind to your own sinfulness. You can't even see it. Your pride and your customs have made you callous and they are leading you into a disaster. Jerusalem and the temple will be destroyed in a fire which won't be put out, and if you

---

7. Ellis, *AD70 and the End of the World*, under heading "Vespian and Titus: A Father and Son Demolition Team" in "Chapter 9: The Great Tribulation," Kindle location 889.

don't turn around and repent from your violent ways, you too will be destroyed in that fire as well." Tragically, all Jesus warned of came true in AD 70. N. T. Wright does a good job of setting Jesus' Gehenna warnings within the context of the looming destruction of Jerusalem. Wright describes the background to Gehenna this way:

> The point is that when Jesus was warning his hearers about Gehenna, he was not, as a general rule, telling them that unless they repented in this life they would burn in the next one. As with God's kingdom, so with its opposite: it is on earth that things matter, not somewhere else. His message to his contemporaries was stark and (as we would say today) political. Unless they turned back from their hopeless and rebellious dreams of establishing God's kingdom in their own terms, not least through armed revolt against Rome, then the Roman juggernaut would do what large, greedy, and ruthless empires have always done to smaller countries (not least in the Middle East) whose resources they covet or whose strategic location they are anxious to guard. Rome would turn Jerusalem into a hideous, stinking extension of its own smoldering rubbish heap. When Jesus said, "Unless you repent, you will all likewise perish," that is the primary meaning he had in mind.[8]

The Gehenna warnings of Jesus make sense within their historical context. Jesus saw how the path of sin and violence was the path of destructive rebellion against God. Jesus' hearers would not have heard these warnings as referring to some otherworldly afterlife. In their typical Jewish way of thinking at that time they would have heard these warnings within their world in which Gehenna was a literal valley whose name had become a symbol of judgment and destruction. When the Jews of Jesus' day heard Jesus talking about Gehenna they would not likely have thought about some unearthly place of endless torture. They would have thought about that cursed valley of judgment and destruction just south of the city walls of Jerusalem. We shouldn't minimize the seriousness of the threat of Gehenna, nor the destruction it represented; however, neither should we make Gehenna into something it didn't automatically refer to at the time of Jesus—namely an endless, other-worldly, fiery torture pit.

---

8. Wright, *Surprised by Hope*, 176.

The Sheep and the Goats

Having considered this background to Jesus' warnings about Gehenna, let's now turn to a text which does not mention Gehenna but which is often the main text cited to argue that hell is everlasting torment. The parable of the sheep and the goats, found in Matthew 25:31–46, at first glance, does seem to endorse the idea of a place of torment which lasts forever. However, once the original languages and contexts are considered, this interpretation is not necessarily as obvious as it might initially seem. The part of the parable used to argue for eternal torment is found in the last sentence. Here is the entire parable, found in Matthew 25:31–46:

> "When the Son of Man comes in his glory, and all the angels with him, he will sit on his glorious throne. All the nations will be gathered before him, and he will separate the people one from another as a shepherd separates the sheep from the goats. He will put the sheep on his right and the goats on his left.
>
> "Then the King will say to those on his right, 'Come, you who are blessed by my Father; take your inheritance, the kingdom prepared for you since the creation of the world. For I was hungry and you gave me something to eat, I was thirsty and you gave me something to drink, I was a stranger and you invited me in, I needed clothes and you clothed me, I was sick and you looked after me, I was in prison and you came to visit me.'
>
> "Then the righteous will answer him, 'Lord, when did we see you hungry and feed you, or thirsty and give you something to drink? When did we see you a stranger and invite you in, or needing clothes and clothe you? When did we see you sick or in prison and go to visit you?'
>
> "The King will reply, 'Truly I tell you, whatever you did for one of the least of these brothers and sisters of mine, you did for me.'
>
> "Then he will say to those on his left, 'Depart from me, you who are cursed, into the eternal fire prepared for the devil and his angels. For I was hungry and you gave me nothing to eat, I was thirsty and you gave me nothing to drink, I was a stranger and you did not invite me in, I needed clothes and you did not clothe me, I was sick and in prison and you did not look after me.' "They also will answer, 'Lord, when did we see you hungry or thirsty or a stranger or needing clothes or sick or in prison, and did not help you?'
>
> "He will reply, 'Truly I tell you, whatever you did not do for one of the least of these, you did not do for me.'
>
> "Then they will go away to eternal punishment, but the righteous to eternal life."

The last verse of the parable is the single most important passage used to support belief in an eternal hell where God forever punishes the guilty. The key verse is Matthew 25:46, which reads in most English translations of the Bible something like, "And these will go away into eternal punishment, but the righteous into eternal life." Jesus here suggests there will indeed be a division which comes. Some will go into eternal punishment. Some will go into eternal life. However, the Greek words often translated as eternal and punishment have shades of meaning which can throw a different light on the interpretation of this all-important verse.

Two Important Greek Words: *Aion* and *Kolasis*

In the Greek of the New Testament the word often translated as eternal is *aionian*. *Aionian* is an adjective based on the noun *aion*, which can have a variety of meanings. To say *aionian* always means "eternal" is an oversimplification. Many times in the New Testament the word *aion* simply refers to an age or a period of time in the past or present or the future. There are ages which have passed and there are ages which are yet to come. With regard to the ages yet to come, we can see them referred to in Ephesians 2:7. In this passage Paul tells about the *ages* yet to come, in which God will show the immeasurable riches of his grace in Christ. According to Ephesians 2:7 there is not a single age to come, but rather ages still to come.

Since the word *aionion* is an adjective based on the word *aion*, it's important to know how in Greek, especially when thinking of time, different objects have different *aions*. For instance, the *aion* of a tree is different from the *aion* of a flower, is different from the *aion* of God. The *aion* of something is just a way of saying how long it lasts. Therefore, to say that the life of God and the punishment of God are both *aionian* is really only to say that God's life and God's punishment both endure, or last, as long as is consistent with what they are. Anyone who studies the Greek noun *aion* and the adjective *aionian* will quickly discover how versatile the word *aionian* is depending on its context. To say *aionian* always means "that which lasts forever" is a gross oversimplification.

The next word which needs to be considered is the word translated as "punishment" in Matthew 25:46. This word comes from the Greek word *kolasis*. The Greek word *kolasis* has its background in the world of horticulture. It originally had to do with pruning or trimming back plants in order to make them healthier. To subject a plant to *kolasis* was to remove from the plant that which was dead and diseased so the plant might grow back properly. To subject a person to *kolasis* would be to accomplish a similar purpose, to remove that which is dead and diseased so the person may be put back on the right track. The New Testament scholar William Barclay had this to say about the background of *kolasis*: "The Greek word for punishment is kolasis, which was not originally an ethical word at all. It originally meant the pruning of trees to make them grow better. I think it is true to say that in all Greek secular literature kolasis is never used of anything but remedial punishment."[9]

Yet another aspect of the parable is that the goats are not adult goats but kid-goats (*eriphos* in the Greek). The same kid-goat appears in the parable of the prodigal son as well. The older brother complains that his father had splurged and given the fatted calf for the younger brother while never even giving him a young goat (*eriphon* in the Greek) so he could celebrate with his friends. In the Matthew 25 parable the fundamental contrast being made between the sheep and the goats is then arguably between the mature and the immature—between the fatted calf and the young goat in the parable of the prodigal son, and between the sheep and the kid-goats in Matthew 25. About this contrast Alex Smith comments, "The Greek word *eriphos/eriphon*, which gets translated in the parable as 'goats,' is translated as 'young goat' in the Parable of the Prodigal Son. This is the only other occurrence in the New Testament but as there are about 100 occurrences in other ancient texts, most Greek dictionaries say the word means 'young goats' or 'kids.' . . . Because of this, I think Jesus is deliberately contrasting mature sheep with kids who need a lot of maturing."[10]

Taking all of this into consideration can change one's perspective on the *aionion kolasin* into which the kid-goats are said to go in Matthew 25:46. This verse could be read to mean that the immature goats who go into judgment will have to endure a time, or an age, or ages, of God's corrective presence for the purpose of bringing them ultimately back to themselves and to God. In this way of thinking, *aionion kolasin* is understood to be God's determined corrective punishment, which is to be taken seriously, and seriously to be avoided. We shouldn't want anything to do with *aionion kolasin*, since it will be a rigorous, difficult, searching, unrelenting experience which will continue until its purposes are fulfilled. However, even

---

9. Barclay, *Spiritual Autobiography*, 66.
10. Smith, "Parable of the Sheep."

aionion kolasin, from this point of view, would not be a completely hopeless situation. It would be the means by which a loving God increasingly impresses the necessary consequences of sin upon wayward children—not for the purposes of sending them away forever, but for the ultimate purpose of bringing them back home.

Matthew 25:46 and the Judgment of the Nations

Another aspect of Matthew 25:46 which complicates the interpretation of the parable is that Jesus' whole parable of the sheep and the kid-goats may not be directed at individual people at all, but rather at the nations. In other words, at first glance one might think the parable is about Jesus judging individual people based on whether they showed compassion towards the poor. But upon a closer reading of the whole passage, it may be Jesus intended his teaching to be a warning directed at the nations, especially with regard to how they treated his followers.

In the beginning of the parable Jesus describes how all the nations, literally all the *ethnos*, will be gathered before the judge. At that time, these *ethnos* will be judged by how they have treated Jesus' brothers and sisters. When Jesus is speaking of his brothers and sisters, of whom is he speaking? Most likely Jesus is here referring to his followers, to the ones he affectionately called his "little flock."[11] According to Jesus' warning, how the *ethnos*, or the nations, treat his brothers and sisters, his little flock, amounts to the way they have unknowingly treated him. What Jesus meant by the parable of the sheep and the goats may have been something like, "Nations and peoples, as you treat one of these brothers and sisters of mine badly, you treat me badly. And as you treat one of them well, you treat me well. Be warned. Mistreating me by mistreating my brothers and sisters will result in God's judgment."

The parable of the sheep and the goats in Matthew 25 is a fascinating study. Is the parable directed at individual people or at the nations, or at both at once? The parable makes us all pause and consider how we are living our lives. It contains serious warnings. However, I believe even these warnings can be seen to fit within a biblical view of God who includes all and who intends to ultimately bring all nations and peoples back home to God through a process of purification from evil.

11. "Do not be afraid, little flock, for your Father has been pleased to give you the kingdom" (Luke 12:32).

The Narrow Way

Jesus often speaks about people not finding something very important. In the following passage, from Matthew 7:13–14, Jesus warns about a hard road and a narrow gate which few find. The advice Jesus gives is, "Enter through the narrow gate; for the gate is wide and the road is easy that leads to destruction, and there are many who take it. For the gate is narrow and the road is hard that leads to life, and there are few who find it." Upon first reading, this passage can seem very discouraging. Was Jesus trying to say only a few people will ever make it into heaven because the gate is so narrow and the road so hard? However, upon closer inspection, we find Jesus was not speaking here to people about the future, but about the present moment. When Jesus taught about the kingdom of God he described the kingdom as a present reality which most people of his day were missing.

In this passage from Matthew all of the verbs are in the present tense, something we can't see unless we look at the original Greek text. If we take into account the present-tenseness of the verbs, suddenly Jesus' teaching has a striking sense of immediacy to it. A more literal translation of this text might be, "Enter through the narrow gate, for the gate is wide and the road is easy which is leading away into destruction, and there are many who are entering through it. For the gate is narrow and the road is hard that is leading the way into life, and few are those who are finding it." When we read this passage in the present tense we see how Jesus was describing something taking place right in front of him. Jesus had come to show people the way to enter the enduring life of God's kingdom which Jesus was declaring now to be present among them. But, as Jesus observed, entering the kingdom now required too much of them. So instead they walked the path of destruction.

The word translated as "destruction" here is a form of the Greek word *apollumi*. It is important to note that *apollumi* does not necessarily mean to cause to cease to exist completely. For instance, in Luke 15, Jesus tells of a shepherd with one hundred sheep. One of the sheep, in being separated from the shepherd, is literally said to be in a state of destruction. But when the lost sheep is found it is no longer destroyed, no longer in a state of destruction. It is restored. The lost sheep is one of three things which are in a state of lostness, or destruction. There is a lost sheep, a lost coin, and a lost son. In Luke 15, the lost sheep, the lost coin, and the lost son are all restored from their state of destruction when they are found.

When we walk the easy path away from Jesus and the kingdom of God we are following the path of destruction. We experience more destructive consequences the further down the path we go. But experiencing this kind of destruction doesn't mean going out of existence altogether. Jesus is the Good Shepherd. He won't let any of his sheep be in a state of destruction forever. Even if Jesus will finally completely rescue all of us from the destruction we bring on ourselves, it's still much, much, much better not to be destroying ourselves on the wide path, even though it is so easy to do.

The Rich Man and Lazarus

Jesus' parable about a rich man and a poor man named Lazarus is another passage which is used to suggest that all will not be saved. This parable, found in Luke 16:19–31, features a wealthy man who ignores the plight of a poor beggar. It also features an uncrossable chasm which seems to separate the rich man and the beggar in eternity. Here is the parable:

> "There was a rich man who was dressed in purple and fine linen and lived in luxury every day. At his gate was laid a beggar named Lazarus, covered with sores and longing to eat what fell from the rich man's table. Even the dogs came and licked his sores.
>
> "The time came when the beggar died and the angels carried him to Abraham's side. The rich man also died and was buried. In Hades, where he was in torment, he looked up and saw Abraham far away, with Lazarus by his side. So he called to him, 'Father Abraham, have pity on me and send Lazarus to dip the tip of his finger in water and cool my tongue, because I am in agony in this fire.'
>
> "But Abraham replied, 'Son, remember that in your lifetime you received your good things, while Lazarus received bad things, but now he is comforted here and you are in agony. And besides all this, between us and you a great chasm has been set in place, so that those who want to go from here to you cannot, nor can anyone cross over from there to us.'
>
> "He answered, 'Then I beg you, father, send Lazarus to my family, for I have five brothers. Let him warn them, so that they will not also come to this place of torment.'
>
> "Abraham replied, 'They have Moses and the Prophets; let them listen to them.'
>
> "'No, father Abraham,' he said, 'but if someone from the dead goes to them, they will repent.'

"He said to him, 'If they do not listen to Moses and the Prophets, they will not be convinced even if someone rises from the dead.'"

Because of the way the Bible was originally translated into English, the parable of the rich man and Lazarus was understood to support the idea of a hell from which there is no return. In the King James Version, the word used to translate "Hades" (the place where the rich man went), was the word "hell," bringing with it all of its medieval baggage. However, the word "Hades" is really there in the original language, and now most modern English versions of the Bible have changed their translations to reflect this. As a case in point, in 2011 the NIV (New International Version), a leading translation among evangelical Christians, changed their translation of this word in the parable. Before 2011, evangelical readers of the NIV would have read in their Bibles that the rich man went to hell, which was on the other side of a great chasm no one could ever cross. After 2011, those same readers would now read that the rich man went to Hades. And that's significant because this parable, with its supposed reference to hell, has long been used to defend the idea of the eternal separation of the damned.

One of the reasons for choosing the NIV as the primary translation for this book was to show how English translations of the Bible must continue to advance and adjust their translations in order to be more accurate. In order to get a better sense of the original text it's helpful to consult more literal translations such as *Young's Literal*, or *The Concordant Literal*, and especially David Bentley Hart's *The New Testament: A Translation*. It also helps to consult online interlinear versions of the New Testament, which provide the original Greek text, identify verb tenses, and help with grammar. The parable of the rich man and Lazarus is a case in point because it's helpful to know that it was Hades and not hell to which the rich man had been confined.

As important as the distinction between hell and Hades is, the parable itself, does not seem to have description of the afterlife as its main purpose. The main thrust of the parable is a stern warning from Jesus about the danger of being caught up in material wealth. The reason the rich man is in Hades is because of his opulent lifestyle and his insensitivity to the suffering of the poor. But even in Hades, the rich man does not seem to have yet fully learned his lesson. He realizes he is in trouble, but still seems to think he is in charge. He wants Lazarus to be sent to him as a servant to quench his thirst. He wants messengers to be sent to his family to warn them. But he is told there is a cavern which none can cross separating him from the world of the living. In this parable Jesus uses the fiery setting of Hades in order to make a point. Jesus often used shocking language to jolt his listeners into hearing what he had to say. When Jesus taught about judgment he used the common terms of his day. In the ancient world, Hades was considered the abode of the dead. It was thought to be a kind of holding tank prior to final judgment. It was a place where people entered into the consequences of their earthly actions. But Hades was not understood to be an eternal destination. In the parable of the rich man and Lazarus the main point Jesus is making is about the importance of sensitivity to the poor. Now we turn to another fiery text which seems to suggest that God's final judgment means some will be lost forever.

The Blazing Furnace

Fire is one of the images Jesus provocatively incorporated into his warnings about future judgment. But if we look carefully at the surrounding details we can see that the fire of judgment is a special kind of fire which produces intense awareness and remorse. A good example of this is Jesus' teaching about a blazing furnace found in Matthew 13:49–50. In this passage Jesus warns, "This is how it will be at the end of the age. The angels will come and separate the wicked from the righteous and throw them into the blazing furnace, where there will be weeping and gnashing of teeth." Jesus speaks here of the wicked being thrown into a blazing furnace, which produces weeping and gnashing of teeth. However, elsewhere Jesus speaks of the wicked being thrown into outer darkness, which also produces weeping and gnashing of teeth (see Matt 8:12; 22:13; and 25:30). The point is not to take either the fire or the darkness literally. The point is that God's judgments, whether characterized as fire or darkness, produce intense remorse. They are a direct, grueling encounter with the full force of truth. The length of the judgment is not described. It's neither characterized as brief nor unending. It's the place where unrepentant evil collides with full awareness and full consequence. Everything becomes blindingly clear. Everything that needs to be felt is felt to its necessary depth. It's a place where no one finally gets away with anything.

One of the problems people have with the idea of everyone ultimately making it to heaven is the perception that this means the wicked will never fully understand or fully feel the pain they have caused. They will just get away with it. The image of a blazing furnace which produces weeping and gnashing of teeth certainly counters the idea of anyone getting off easy. Heath Bradley, a minister in the United Methodist Church, in his book *Flames of Love*, tells a story which powerfully illustrates this. Bradley had reached a point in his spiritual journey where he was believing God would ultimately save all. During that same time period he was asked to do spiritual counseling with a man who'd recently been released from prison. The man did not want to go to church because he had offended against children. But he wanted to meet with a minister because he'd become a Christian in prison and was looking for help in his spiritual life. At first Bradley did not want to meet with him. But then he realized he'd be a hypocrite if he really believed that the power of grace to restore was greater than the power of sin to destroy. He eventually agreed to meet with the man, even though he was still hesitant. Here is Bradley's recounting of that meeting:

> So the morning came and we met in my office. I was first surprised that he looked normal. I was expecting someone with greasy hair and red eyes, but I got an average-looking farmer in overalls. My next surprise came when we sat down and I began to talk. I have never had a conversation where I felt like the Holy Spirit was in charge as much as this one. As I began to talk to him, I felt an overwhelming love for him. I told him, "You know in your heart that God absolutely hates and weeps over what you have done with your life, but I want you to know in your heart that God has never stopped loving you and that you are God's child." After saying this to him, he began to weep. Through tears and sobs, he told me about a lot of the pain he had experienced in life. He had been horribly abused as a child himself. While in prison he had received numerous beatings. All of his friends had cut their ties with him. Pain, receiving it and inflicting it on others, was the defining feature of his life.
>
> But do you know what he said was the most painful thing he has ever experienced? It wasn't being beaten, raped, or rejected. It was being forgiven. He said that being forgiven by God was the most painful thing he has ever experienced. The experience of being embraced by a divine love in the midst of his sinful mess of a life was for him both the most joyful and, at the same time, most painful thing imaginable for him. Before he opened his heart to the power of God's Spirit, his heart was hard and his mind was darkened. He could do horrible things and not experience sorrow or regret because he was blind to what was really going on. In a very real sense, he did not know what he was doing. Indeed, evil

and sin always involve a deep kind of self-deception and ignorance. Recall that when Jesus was hanging on the cross, he prayed, "Father forgive them, for they do not know what they are doing" (Luke 23:34). But as God's Spirit began to take a hold of him, his heart began to soften and his mind began to clear. He was now seeing and feeling for the first time the horror of what he had done. And it hurt like hell.

I tell this story because it shows that forgiveness is not the equivalent of getting off the hook without facing any consequences.[12]

As this story illustrates so well, forgiveness is not exemption from consequences. God's judgments are meant to produce remorse and repentance, and ultimately to awaken the innate desire for faith. The blazing fire of God's judgment, as well as the terrifying outer darkness, are places where there is no escape from the bitterness of the truth. God's goodness is no safe haven for the unrepentant. Since God's ultimate goal is reconciliation, this forces God's proximate goal to be creating judgments which are equal to the seriousness of the sin which has been committed. There can be no reconciliation without full recognition of the damage the sin has done.

Being Disowned

Two warnings found in the New Testament demonstrate very well the necessity of repentance before there can be full reconciliation. The first is a warning from Jesus about the consequences of denying him. This warning, found in Matthew 10:33, goes as follows, "But whoever disowns me before others, I will disown before my Father in heaven." Denying Jesus brings serious consequences. The verb translated here as "disown" is *arnesetai* and it occurs only one time in the New Testament. Sometimes it is also translated as "deny." The tense of this verb implies an ongoing action which triggers an ongoing response. The Concordant Literal Version does a good job capturing this ongoing sense. It reads, "Yet, who should ever be disowning Me in front of men, I also will be disowning him in front of My Father Who is in the heavens." In other words, as long as someone is denying Jesus, Jesus is denying them before the Father. And the reverse is also true. Once someone stops denying Jesus, Jesus stops denying them before the Father.

---

12. Bradley, *Flames of Love*, 46–47.

Consider the case of Peter, who disowned or denied Jesus three times on the night Jesus was arrested. Peter denied Jesus not once, not twice, but three times, saying repeatedly, "I don't know him." If Jesus' teaching about denying him means that if anybody ever denies him then there is absolutely no chance for forgiveness, then how do we understand Jesus forgiving Peter? Denying Jesus doesn't result in eternal rejection. However, as long as we are denying Jesus, we will not be able to experience reconciliation with God. This same dynamic of reciprocal rejection is at play in a second warning. This warning, found in Matthew 12:30–32, regards the seriousness of speaking against the Holy Spirit. It reads, "Whoever is not with me is against me, and whoever does not gather with me scatters. And so I tell you, every kind of sin and slander can be forgiven, but blasphemy against the Spirit will not be forgiven. Anyone who speaks a word against the Son of Man will be forgiven, but anyone who speaks against the Holy Spirit will not be forgiven, either in this age or in the age to come."

Notice Jesus' reference here to time as a series of ages. He speaks of this age and of the age to come. What Jesus is saying is that as long as we are denying the work of the Holy Spirit in any age, be it this age or any coming age, we cannot be forgiven—cannot be fully reconciled to God. The work of the Holy Spirit is so central that it must be received. Rejecting the Holy Spirit is not something that can ever be forgiven in the sense that it is a non-negotiable. One can't be fully reconciled to God while at the same time rejecting the Holy Spirit of God.

A good illustration of this principle is found in Jesus' parable about an unforgiving servant in Matthew 18. In that parable a merciful king forgives his servant's incredibly enormous debt. Then the man, after having been forgiven this huge debt, turns around and refuses to forgive a tiny debt owed to him. The king, upon finding out about this, orders the debt of this merciless man to be *un*forgiven. The debt is so huge that the man has no way to pay it back. Consequently, the king sentences the man to be tortured until he paid back all he owed. In the mind of Jesus, unforgiveness breeds unforgiveness. Rejection of the Holy Spirit breeds rejection both in this age, and in the age to come. This doesn't mean that the rejection will last forever. It is, however, something which is very serious and which must be resolved before reconciliation can fully can take place.

Perishing for Lack of Belief

Another passage which deals with rejection is John 3:16. It seems to imply that those who don't believe in Jesus in this life will be forever rejected after death. It reads, "For God so loved the world that he gave his one and only Son, that whoever believes in him shall not perish but have eternal life." The NIV, like most other English translations, for the purpose of readability, does not translate the verbs in this passage in the present tense in which they were written in the original Greek. Therefore, when most people read this passage it says to them something like, "God gave his son, and everyone who has believed in him will get eternal life, and everyone who hasn't believed in him will be eternally rejected." Because the rejection they experience is described as perishing, this text is often quoted by those who believe hell is complete annihilation.

But consider the way the Concordant Literal Version (CLV) translates John 3:16. It preserves the present tense of the verbs, and also uses English words which are more closely equivalent to the Greek. Here is John 3:16 in the CLV: "For thus God loves the world, so that He gives His only-begotten Son, that everyone who is believing in Him should not be perishing, but may be having life eonian." Notice how when the verb tenses are taken into account, everything in John 3:16 is happening in the present tense. God loves the world. God gives his Son. Everyone who is believing is not perishing but entering into eonian life. The CLV uses the English word "eonian" to translate the Greek word *aionian*. Those who are not entering God's eonian, or *aionian*, kind of life are perishing. The word for "perishing" here is based on the Greek word *apollumi*. This kind of perishing is the withering which takes place when we are separated from God's true life. However, this withering does not mean ceasing to exist altogether. As we have already seen, in Jesus' parables in Luke 15 about the lost sheep, lost coin, and lost son, all three were in a state of perishing described by the Greek word *apollumi*. Even though the sheep, the coin, and the son were all in a state of perishing, they never went out of existence altogether. Instead they were experiencing the withering which comes from not being connected to the eonian, or *aionian*, or eternal life of God.

What John 3:16 does is to make an observation. Some are becoming believing ones and therefore receiving right now the *aionian* or eonian life of God which comes through ongoing confidence and trust in the Son. Others are not believing and therefore not yet receiving this kind of life. They are in a state of withering, or lostness, or perishing, because, although they are existing, they are perishing and withering until they are connected to the life that really is life. Because of their lack of faith, they are not able to experience the *aionian* God-life in which they have already been included. Although they are included in it by grace, they cannot experience it if they aren't having faith, and so they are perishing rather than really living.

Everlasting Destruction

A passage from Paul's writings in 2 Thessalonians speaks about this same kind of destruction. In 2 Thessalonians 1:9 Paul warns, "They will be punished with everlasting destruction and shut out from the presence of the Lord and from the glory of his might." This verse, as it is usually translated into English, seems to say those who are being punished are being put in an unrecoverable state. They are seemingly shut out from God forever by an everlasting destruction which comes from God. However, there is another way of looking at this text in the original Greek. Young's Literal Translation renders the verse as saying the guilty "shall suffer justice—destruction age-during—from the face of the Lord, and from the glory of his strength." In other words, what's happening here is that there is a destruction coming from God towards the guilty. The really crucial translation question with this verse has to do with how to interpret the Greek word *apo* which is like our English word *from*. Sometimes, depending on context, our word "from" can mean "coming from" or it can mean "away from." Also, the word translated as "eternal" is the Greek word *aion*, which can also mean an "age," or mean "of God" when it's referring to God. Therefore, this verse could also be taken to mean that the guilty will experience enduring destruction which comes from the face of God. However, it doesn't necessarily connote a permanent separation from God.

No More Chances after Death?

According to Hebrews 9:26–27, "[Christ] has appeared once for all at the culmination of the ages to do away with sin by the sacrifice of himself. Just as people are destined to die once, and after that to face judgment . . . ." In the discussion about eternal destinies, the phrase from this verse about people being destined to die once and after that to face judgment is often used to defeat the idea that there can be postmortem opportunities for salvation. However, what this verse states does not conflict with the final salvation of all because judgment is part of the path towards salvation for those who need it. The context of the verse has to do with Christ's unique, unrepeatable sacrifice of himself. Whereas the sacrifices outlined in the Old Testament had to be repeated, Christ's sacrifice was sufficient for all time. The main point of this verse has to do with the uniqueness of Christ's sacrifice. As Stephen Jonathan notes in *Grace beyond the Grave*,

> The point of this verse is to illustrate the once-for-all aspect of the work of Christ, as opposed to the unfinished nature of the Old Testament sacrificial system, and is not a reference to personal eschatology. Whilst arguments from silence are always uncertain, it is nevertheless of interest that biblical commentaries do not choose to use this verse in the manner that it is often quoted in contemporary evangelicalism, and make no reference to this verse as referring to death being the end of human probation. The writer of Hebrews uses this reference to show that human death is a once-for-all occurrence as a consequence of sin, so too Christ died once-for-all to take away the sins of many people.[13]

Even if we imagine a possibility for salvation after death, the importance of death as a significant event should not be minimized. There should be no delay in spiritual growth rationalized on the basis that whatever needs to be dealt with will be dealt with after death. If we accept that the main point of life is spiritual progress then we should make the most spiritual progress we can in this life; not because we will be permanently rejected if we don't, but because we are being perfectly loved. If the ultimate purpose of judgment is to set things right, then we should enthusiastically and gratefully open ourselves now to whatever can be set right before we die. The generosity of God's love should not make us stingy in our response, just the reverse. If we die once and then face judgment on that life, then our primary project in this life is to get as close as we can to being formed in the perfect love and faith which Christ himself exemplified.

We've now covered a good portion of the judgment texts found in the New Testament. But we have yet to address the book of Revelation. Its judgment scenes become a central point of discussion in the debate about eternal destinies. And it is to this mysterious book we turn next.

---

13. Jonathan, *Grace beyond the Grave*, 89.

5

The Book of Revelation

> That the lake of fire represents purgatorial suffering . . . seems clear from that magnificent vision in Revelation 21 of the New Jerusalem with its gates never closing and a continuous stream of incoming traffic.
>
> —Thomas Talbott[1]

Hope within Warning

WHEN CONSIDERING THE JUDGMENTS of God, the book of Revelation occupies a special place in the Bible. Revelation is often characterized as the ultimate book of warning which paints a crystal-clear picture of the final judgment of God—one in which the righteous and the wicked are permanently separated. Yet there is also a very hopeful and inclusive aspect to the book of Revelation. In the final chapters there is a vision of the new Jerusalem whose gates are never shut. Through these gates will come the glory and honor of all the nations. Inside the city there is the tree of life whose leaves are for the healing of the nations. All of the unworthy are outside the walls of the city. An invitation goes out to them to come and drink the free gift of the water of life.

I'll give more attention later to Revelation's final vision of the new Jerusalem with its forever open gates, but before that, it's helpful to back up and take a broader approach to this unique book. The dramatic images within the book of Revelation are provocative and challenging. This makes Revelation the hardest book of the New Testament to understand.

---

1. Talbott, *Inescapable Love of God*, 186.

Yet there is an approach to it which helps make sense of it within its original historical context.

The Book of Revelation as Apocalyptic Writing

When I approach the book of Revelation, the first thing I take into consideration is that the book of Revelation is most likely an example of Christian apocalyptic writing. When I first started reading the book of Revelation, because it was so unusual, I didn't know what to make of its strange imagery. I had no context for it. However, that all began to change once I learned that the book of Revelation is considered by many scholars to be an example of apocalyptic writing, which was an entire genre of writing in the ancient world. There are many examples of Jewish and Christian apocalypses both before and after Jesus' earthly life. An apocalypse is a highly symbolic form of writing which pulls back the curtains of the hidden spiritual realms to reveal the mysteries which are to come. Apocalyptic writing was a response to great persecution. The message of apocalyptic writing was straightforward—evil will be defeated and good will win out in the end.

The immediate purpose of the book of Revelation was to encourage persecuted Christians not to give up their faith since their rescue was soon at hand. The nearness of their expected rescue can be seen in the first sentence of the book of Revelation, which reads, "The revelation from Jesus Christ, which God gave him to show his servants what must soon take place" (Rev 1:1). Throughout Revelation the reader is told that "the time is near" (Rev 1:3); that believers "should hold fast" until he comes (Rev 2:25 and 3:11); that it will only be a "little longer" (Rev 6:11); that all "must soon take place" (Rev 22:6); that the Lord is "coming soon" (Rev 22:7); to not seal up the words of this book because "the time is near" (Rev 22:10); that Jesus is "coming soon" (Rev 22:12); and then finally at very end there is Jesus' promise, "Surely I am coming soon" (Rev 22:20). Whatever the book of Revelation may ultimately mean, its immediate purpose was to be an inspiration to Christians undergoing persecution by the Roman Empire.

Because Revelation was set in a time of great persecution, we are not surprised to find it contains stern warnings about the consequences of leaving the faith. Revelation 14:9–11 is a good example of this. It reads:

> A third angel followed them and said in a loud voice: "If anyone worships the beast and its image and receives its mark on their forehead or on their hand, they too, will drink the wine of God's

fury, which has been poured full strength into the cup of his wrath. They will be tormented with burning sulfur in the presence of the holy angels and of the Lamb. And the smoke of their torment will rise for ever and ever. There will be no rest day or night for those who worship the beast and its image, or for anyone who receives the mark of its name."

The fate of those who worship the beast is to be tormented with burning sulfur in the presence of Jesus and the angels. Then we are told the smoke of their torment will last forever and ever. But what can it mean to say that the smoke of their torment will last forever and ever? If it lasts forever, then why add to forever by saying forever *and* ever? How can there be an ever after forever? Something has been lost in translation. The solution comes when we look into the ancient understanding of time as something which moved forward in a series of coming ages, not in a series of coming eternities. Young's Literal Translation more accurately captures this phenomenon in by translating this verse literally as, "and the smoke of their torment doth go up to ages of ages." The phrase "ages of ages" gives us a sense of a very long, but not necessarily an endless, period of time. A distinction can also be made between their torment and the smoke of their torment in vs. 11. It may be that what endures is not their torment, but the smoke of their torment. If the smoke of their torment represents the consequences of their actions, then it could be that the consequences, or the effects, of their punishment may somehow continuously follow after them.

What's happening to these people is that they are being punished with an eternal, or more literally an *aionian*, punishment. But let's remember the fate of Sodom. According to the New Testament in Jude 1:7, Sodom serves as an example of "those who suffer the punishment of eternal [literally *aionian*] fire." Yet Ezekiel, as part of his hopeful prophecy of the eventual restoration of Jerusalem, goes on to make the stunning prophecy that God will restore even the fortunes of Sodom. In Ezekiel 16:53 we read, "However, I will restore the fortunes of Sodom and her daughters and of Samaria and her daughters, and your fortunes along with them." On the one hand, I want to take as seriously as I can the threat of entering into an eternal, or *aionian*, punishment from God. On the other hand, I also see in the Bible the possibility of restoration even on the other side of that kind of punishment from God.

Another passage from Revelation which seems to suggest a possible absolute end for those judged unworthy is found in Revelation 20:15, which reads, "Anyone whose name was not found written in the book of life was thrown into the lake of fire." The lake of fire plays a central role in Revelation, but it has some surprising qualities.

The Lake of Fire

Chapter 20 in the book of Revelation covers lots of ground. Satan is imprisoned for a thousand years. The Christian martyrs who lost their lives for their faith are raised from the dead to reign with Christ for that thousand-year period. Then, after the thousand years has passed, Satan is released from prison and he goes about deceiving all the nations. A great army follows Satan in a war against God's people. Fire comes down from heaven and consumes the enemy. The devil is thrown into the lake of fire, along with the beast and the false prophet who had led the rebellion against God. Then the devil, the beast, and the false prophet are tormented in the lake of fire forever and ever (literally . . . to the ages of the ages). Then there is a great white throne, and all of the dead are standing before it. Everybody is there. The sea gives up her dead. It is said that Death and Hades give up their dead. And then all are judged. Then Death and Hades themselves are thrown into the lake of fire. And then we read in Revelation 20:15 that anyone whose name was not found written in the book of life was thrown into the lake of fire, which is understood to be the second death.

By the end of the twentieth chapter of Revelation it seems as if everyone whose names were not written in the book of life are now all in the second death in the lake of fire. Then we get to chapter 21 of Revelation. Here we are told that after all of this has taken place a new heaven and earth will come into being. The old heaven and earth have passed away, and along with it the sea, for the sea is no more (Rev 21:1). Then the new Jerusalem, prepared as a bride adorned for her husband, descends from the new heaven to the new earth in the form of a super massive cube 1,500 miles long, wide, and high (see Rev 21:16). Everyone whose name is written in the book of life gets to come into the new Jerusalem. Everyone else will be consigned to the lake of fire. Now at this point it really looks like it's all over for everyone that didn't get their names in the book of life. They were thrown in the lake of fire in Revelation 20:15 before the arrival of the new Jerusalem, and their place in the lake of fire is reaffirmed in Revelation 21:8. But then we come to Revelation chapter 22, and here in we find a curiously hopeful scene.

The Invitation from the Spirit and the Bride

In Revelation 22:14–17, we read about an invitation given from the Spirit and the bride. The invitation reads:

> "Blessed are those who wash their robes, that they may have the right to the tree of life and may go through the gates into the city. Outside are the dogs, those who practice magic arts, the sexually immoral, the murderers, the idolaters and everyone who loves and practices falsehood.
>
> "I, Jesus, have sent my angel to give you this testimony for the churches. I am the Root and the Offspring of David, and the bright Morning Star."
>
> The Spirit and the bride say, "Come!" And let the one who hears say, "Come!" Let the one who is thirsty come; and let the one who wishes take the free gift of the water of life.

The new Jerusalem has come down from heaven. The church, symbolized as Christ's bride, is gathered into the city. We are told, however, there are still people outside the gates. They are a mighty sorry lot. The Spirit and the Bride issue an invitation to come in and drink the free gift of the water of life. To whom is this invitation given? Is it possible this invitation is being given to all the unworthy people outside the gates? Robin Parry, in his book *The Evangelical Universalist*, argues that it is. And he sees this reaffirmed as well in Revelation 5:13, which reads, "Then I heard every creature in heaven and on earth and under the earth and on the sea, and all that is in them, saying: 'To him who sits on the throne and to the Lamb be praise and honor and glory and power, for ever and ever!'" Parry also notes that all throughout Revelation we see that the kings of the earth are the enemies of the Lamb. But then in Revelation 21:24 we read, "The nations will walk by its light, and the kings of the earth will bring their splendor into it." Building on the hope Parry observes in such passages, he wonders whether Revelation 22:14–17 might just be describing an ongoing invitation bringing unending hope even to those outside the eternally open gates of the new Jerusalem. Parry writes:

> In John's visionary geography there are only two places one can be located—within the city enclosed in its walls of salvation (Isaiah 60:18) or outside the city in the lake of fire. The gates of this New Jerusalem are never closed. Given that those in the city would have no reason to leave it to enter the lake of fire, why are the doors always open? . . . In the oracle of Isaiah 60 on which this vision

is based we read that the gates were left open for the purpose of allowing the nations to enter (60:11), and that is the case here too: the open doors are not just a symbol of security but primarily a symbol of the God who excludes no one from his presence forever. Not only do the gates offer the opportunity for the lost to enter salvation from the lake of fire, but in John's vision the lost actually avail themselves of this opportunity.[2]

Hope Even in the Lake of Fire?

When interpreting the book of Revelation, a legitimate question arises about the ending of the book. Is there hope for even those who go into the lake of fire? How is it that the unrighteous go into the lake of fire in Revelation 20:15 and then appear outside the gates of the new Jerusalem in Revelation 22:15? Could it be the lake of fire is the lake of God's purifying presence, the place where all illusions, lies, falsehoods, and rationalizations are finally destroyed? Charles Pridgeon, president and founder of the Pittsburg Bible Institute, saw the purifying possibilities of the lake of fire this way:

> The Lake of Fire and Brimstone signifies a fire burning with brimstone; the word "brimstone" or sulfur defines the character of the fire. The word theion translated "brimstone" is exactly the same word theion which means "divine." Sulfur was sacred to the deity among the ancient Greeks; and was used to fumigate, to purify, and to cleanse and to consecrate to the deity; for this purpose they burned it in their incense. In Homer's Iliad (16:228) one is spoken of as purifying a goblet with fire and brimstone. The verb derived from theion is theioo, which means to hallow, to make divine, or to dedicate to a god. (See Liddell and Scott Greek-English Lexicon, 1897 Edition.)
>
> To any Greek, or to any trained in the Greek language, a "lake of fire and brimstone" would mean a "lake of divine purification." The idea of judgment need not be excluded. Divine purification and divine consecration are the plain meaning in ancient Greek. In the ordinary explanation, this fundamental meaning of the word is entirely left out, and nothing but eternal torment is associated with it.[3]

---

2. MacDonald (pen name for Robin Parry), *Evangelical Universalist*, 115.
3. Pridgeon, *Is Hell Eternal?*, 110–11.

As Charles Pridgeon pointed out, sometimes word meanings change from the ancient world to ours. We have been trained to associate brimstone with the fire of eternal torment. In the ancient world brimstone was associated with purification through fire for dedication to God. The book of Revelation is a unique, apocalyptic book which needs to be approached with great care. Yet even in the book of Revelation it's possible to see a message of hope in the midst of its intimidating imagery.

Concluding Thoughts about the Judgment Passages

Over these past two chapters I have demonstrated how the Inclusive approach works through passages of Scripture which seem to go against it. I've looked at judgment passages, and passages about hell, and also at the book of Revelation as a whole. I've tried to show how the Inclusive approach takes judgment seriously while still finding hope for an ultimate restoration of humanity on the other side of judgment in the ages to come. Having reached this point, it's now appropriate to make some general observations about biblical interpretation.

First, no one approach to the Bible is able to reconcile every single passage found in the Bible. Every theology is grounded in Scripture, yet every theology must also struggle with certain passages of Scripture which seem to go against it. The Transactional approach—in arguing that God wants to save all but will not be able to—must deal with Scriptures which suggest that God, being sovereign, should be able to achieve God's own will. The Exclusive approach—in arguing that God saves everyone God wants to save but does not want to save all—must deal with Scriptures which suggest that God does, in fact, desire the salvation of all. The Inclusive approach—in arguing that God wants to and is able to save all—must deal with Scriptures which seem to suggest some will be eternally lost. Since all theologies end up facing passages of Scripture which are hard to deal with, the question is not *if* these passages will be dealt with, but *how*. All theological approaches must face this dilemma. No theology gets a free pass.

The second thing that needs to be said regarding biblical interpretation is about how the character of Jesus should be the final interpretive key. Jesus, according to John's Gospel, is the Word of God made flesh (John 1:14). Jesus is the Word of God in human form, and the Bible bears witness to him. Therefore, Jesus is the ultimate hermeneutic, the ultimate revelatory framework by which we must understand who God is. In her book *Razing Hell*, Sharon Baker Putt states it this way:

> Whether we want to admit it or not, we all put more weight on some Bible verses and passages than on others. In that regard, I'm no different from everyone else. The 1963 Baptist Faith and Message, a confessional statement of the Southern Baptist Convention, declares that one guideline should dictate how we interpret all of Scripture: "The criterion by which the Bible is to be interpreted is Jesus Christ." In other words, up until the year 2000, when the leadership unfortunately took that statement out of the document, the SBC churches read the Bible through Jesus-colored glasses. And as we construct an alternate view of hell and read the Bible through one specific lens, we will choose to pay more attention to verses that more consistently harmonize with the life and teachings of Jesus. As we discussed before, no matter what we believe about the divinity of Jesus, we Christians interpret through this lens because we believe that Jesus most perfectly reveals God to us. Because this is true, the behavior of Jesus mirrors the behavior of God. Jesus tells us himself that if we see him, we see the Father (John 14:6, 9). He also discloses to us that his actions and behaviors are identical to God's; whatever God does, Jesus does the same (5:19). So how can we do anything other than read and interpret the Bible through Jesus-colored glasses—if we want to know God's character and behavior, that is? In order to understand God, we must understand Jesus. In order to develop an accurate picture of the image of God, we need to examine the image of Jesus that the Bible draws for us.[4]

As I read and interpret the Bible through "Jesus-colored glasses" I am hard-pressed to imagine that God will ever give up on anyone. Jesus never diminished the disastrous consequences of sin, but neither did Jesus ever diminish the miraculous power of God to save. As I see God through Jesus, I am persuaded that the judgment of God ultimately fits within the love of God. Maybe if Jesus had never sat at table and eaten with the tax collectors and sinners, I would see it differently. Maybe if Jesus had cast the first stone at the woman caught in adultery, I could believe he would ultimately give up on the lost. But Jesus *did* sit at table with sinners, and he *did not* cast the first stone. Therefore, I can't imagine God doing anything less.

The third thing to be said about biblical interpretation is that we can't lose sight of the overall narrative arc of the Bible. We have to ask what kind

---

4. Putt, *Razing Hell*, 76–77.

of story the Bible is telling. Is the Bible telling a story where God's rebellious creation falls away and then God is never able to fully win it back? Or is the Bible telling a story where God defeats the powers of evil and is finally able to restore everything lost in the fall? About the appropriateness of a triumphant conclusion to the biblical narrative, Robin Parry writes:

> This is a story for which universal salvation seems a fitting ending. Thus, Paul speaks of "the mystery of [God's] will according to his good pleasure, which he purposed in Christ, to be put into effect when the times reach their fulfillment—to bring unity to all things in heaven and on earth under Christ" (Eph. 1: 9–10). All creation is made "for" and oriented "to" God—and it is summed up and brought to its fitting conclusion and destiny in Jesus. Then at Jesus' name every knee will bow—in heaven, and on earth, and under the earth (i.e., the dead)—and every tongue confess him as Lord (Phil. 2:9–11). All will be subject to Christ, and then Christ will subject himself to the Father on behalf of creation, so that God will be "all in all" (1 Cor. 15:28). That is the kind of end I would expect for the biblical story.
>
> Now, we are so used to the traditional story of hell as the final fate of some/many/most people that we usually fail to notice how out of sync it is as a conclusion to this story. Surely we need a very good explanation for this tale ending in tragedy for some/many/most people. What possible reasons could there be for such an unexpected climax? Even if we think we can find an answer to that question (and finding a good answer to it is a major challenge), it is hard to avoid the conclusion that the biblical story told in a non-universalist way ends in a tragic partial failure for God.[5]

Making an overall interpretation of the Bible is a difficult thing to do. There is no single biblical approach that doesn't run into scriptural problems. And so, we must finally ask which biblical approach aligns most closely with the goodness of God, the character of Jesus, and the overall narrative arc of the Bible. On the whole I believe the Inclusive approach offers the best solution. This approach doesn't eliminate judgment from the picture. It allows for potentially ages and ages of judgment. It warns that the judgments of God begin in this world and then increase in intensity beyond this world. However, it argues that the judgments of God ultimately fit within in the loving and triumphant purposes of God for each person and for all of creation.

---

5. Parry, "A Universalist View," 111.

Yet there are still those who are concerned that we not be too confident about God's ability to finally save all. They feel there is just too much mystery surrounding the final judgments of God. And they also want to point out that God, by granting humans the freedom to resist, may not be able to save all in the end. We turn to these concerns next.

6

Mystery and Free Will

> The words *compelle intrare*, compel them to come in, have been so abused by wicked men that we shudder at them; but, properly understood, they plumb the depth of the Divine mercy. The hardness of God is kinder than the softness of men, and His compulsion is our liberation.
>
> —C. S. Lewis[1]

A Theological Impasse?

A COMMON CONCERN ABOUT Christian universalism is that it seems to violate human free will. Can God actually compel humans to be saved when salvation is manifestly something they do not want? And a related issue also presents itself about the need to allow for sufficient mystery around the things of God, especially when it comes to the outcome of final judgment. Like the mythological six-headed monster, Scylla, and the gigantic whirlpool, Charybdis, in Homer's *Odyssey*, the problems surrounding free will and mystery combine to make a set of formidable obstacles which prevent many from reaching a full-blown theology of universal restoration. Kallistos Ware, a bishop in the Orthodox Church, puts the problem this way:

> If the strongest argument in favor of universal salvation is the appeal to divine love, and if the strongest argument on the opposite side is the appeal to human freedom, then we are brought back to the dilemma with which we started: how are we to bring into concord the two principles God is love and Human beings are free? For the time being we cannot do more than hold fast with equal firmness to both principles at once, while admitting the manner of

---

1. Lewis, *Surprised by Joy*, 292.

their ultimate harmonization remains a mystery beyond our present comprehension.[2]

Bishop Ware finds himself on the horns of an impenetrable mystery. On the one hand, God's love compels God to continue to work for our salvation. On the other hand, humans are given the ability to resist God's own salvific goals for each person. This results in what he calls "a mystery beyond our present comprehension." Because of this mystery, Bishop Ware does not see a way in which we may do more than hope for all to be saved in the end. Other theologians of note find themselves in a similar predicament.

The prominent twentieth-century Catholic theologian Hans Urs von Balthasar is another example of one who combined robust hope with necessary restraint. One the one hand he admitted in principle that some might successfully evade God's love forever. On the other hand he also declared that in reality the chances of it actually occurring were infinitely improbable.[3] Of Balthasar, Henry Karlson writes,

> Since he did not know the outcome of the last judgment, Balthasar made it clear he could not know whether or not all will be saved, but he knew his hope had to take into account the possibility of perdition. His hope relied upon the great work of God to reach out to everyone, giving everyone every opportunity to be converted, to have a change of heart, and to be saved. In his theology, perdition can only be had by a complete and utter rejection of the saving work of God.[4]

Among twentieth-century Protestants, Karl Barth held out one of the strongest hopes for a universal salvation, yet he simultaneously refused to conclude that a universal salvation was inevitable. As George Hunsinger notes, Barth makes "a very strong move in the direction of universal salvation while leaving the question open."[5] Again, in Karl Barth we run into a hesitancy to embrace universal salvation outright.

---

2. Ware, *Inner Kingdom*, 214.
3. Balthasar, *Dare We Hope*, 219.
4. Karlson, *Eschatological Judgment*, 20.
5. Hunsinger, *How to Read Karl Barth*, 132.

Hopeful Inclusivism

Because of the nebulous relationship between God's will to save humanity and humanity's ability to resist salvation, some take a view variously called hopeful universalism or hopeful inclusivism. I will use the term "hopeful inclusivism" because of the way this view stresses the full inclusion of all humanity in Christ without insisting this means all will inevitably be saved. Hopeful inclusivism occupies a liminal place in which hope and uncertainty are mysteriously entangled. In this dialectical theological zone there are equally profound reasons to look expectantly towards a universal salvation *and* to stop short of presuming it will inevitably occur. A modern example of this approach is found in William Paul Young, author of *The Shack*. One the one hand, in his book *Lies We Believe about God*, Young writes in favor of universal salvation, stating:

> God does not wait for my choice and then "save me." God has acted decisively and universally for all humankind. Now our daily choice is to either grow and participate in that reality or continue to live in the blindness of our own independence. Are you suggesting that everyone is saved? That you believe in universal salvation? That is exactly what I am saying! This is real good news! It has been blowing people's minds for centuries now. So much so that we often overcomplicate it and get it wrong. Here's the truth: every person who has ever been conceived was included in the death, burial, resurrection, and ascension of Jesus. When Jesus was lifted up, God "dragged" all human beings to Himself (John 12:32). Jesus is the Savior of all humankind, especially believers (1 Timothy 4:10). Further, every single human being is in Christ (John 1:3), and Christ is in them, and Christ is in the Father (John 14:20). When Christ—the Creator in whom the cosmos was created—died, we all died. When Christ rose, we rose (2 Corinthians 5).[6]

However, Young's affirmation of universal salvation stands in tension with his caution that we not presume all will inevitably be saved. In an article published after the release of his book *Lies We Believe about God*, Young further clarified his position on universal salvation, writing:

> No, I don't believe all roads lead to God, but I do believe that God goes down any road to find us—this I stated clearly in The Shack. Otherwise, the Incarnation and the Passion of Jesus would be meaningless.

6. Young, *Lies We Believe about God*, 115.

Yes, I believe that what God accomplished in the power of the Holy Spirit, in Jesus' death, resurrection and ascension affects and includes the entire cosmos and every human being ever conceived. I stated that clearly in Lies We Believe About God.

No, I don't believe in limited atonement, that Jesus died for only a few who God had previously elected. Jesus is the One elected in whom we all died and rose (II Cor 15). We can't build a trusting relationship with grim determinism.

No, I don't believe in a doctrine that holds that every person will ultimately be reconciled full back to God. Yes, I hope that is true. In fact, Colossians asks us to pray for that, and I do.[7]

Hopeful inclusivists, such as William Paul Young and others, affirm our inclusion in the salvation Christ brings, but they see it as being rigidly deterministic to make it a forgone conclusion that every person will be saved in the end. In this view, real relationship with God necessitates the possibility of real rejection of that relationship. Even if all are eventually saved, the possibility for all not to be saved must have existed. Otherwise, as they see it, it would have been impossible for authentic relationship to exist between God and humanity.

Beyond Hopeful Inclusivism

Those who go beyond hopeful inclusivism to Christian universalism go with varying levels of certainty. Robin Parry, in the introduction to his book *The Evangelical Universalist*, holds his Christian universalism with some level of reserve. He describes it this way:

> Some Christians describe themselves as "hopeful universalists." By this they mean that Scripture gives good grounds for real hope that all will be saved, but there is no certainty. Perhaps human freedom or God's sovereign right to determine the future rule out any certainty here. That is not my position. . . . Other Christians are dogmatic universalists. They argue that it is certain that God will save all. I agree but with a qualification. [My] theology . . . is one that espouses a dogmatic universalism, but I must confess to not being 100% certain that it is correct. Thus I am a hopeful dogmatic universalist, a non-dogmatic dogmatic universalist, if you will. All theological systems need to be offered with a degree of humility, and

7. Hazeldine, "Does 'The Shack' Teach Universalism?"

one that departs significantly from the mainstream Christian tradition calls for even more. I hope to show that, in fact, universalism is not a major change to the tradition and that it actually enables us to hold key elements of the tradition together better than traditional doctrines of hell. Nevertheless, arrogance is out of place.[8]

While Robin Parry incorporates a certain amount of reserve into his non-dogmatic dogmatic approach, David Bentley Hart approaches his case for Christian universalism without any reserve whatsoever. Parry presents Christian universalism as a view which is not a major change to what has become the mainstream Christian tradition. Hart considers what has become the mainstream Christian tradition to be morally disjointed and undeserving of adherence, especially in the Western church under the influence of Augustine. For Hart, the Christian universalist approach is much more than an option to be humbly considered—it's the only logically possible approach to the Christian faith in which God may be rightly said to be good. In his daring book *That All Shall Be Saved*, Hart expresses his views starkly, declaring himself *not* to be a "seeker tentatively and timidly groping his way toward some anxious, uncertain, fragile hope."[9] He then elaborates on his absolute convictions, stating:

> Unlike, say, the great Hans Urs von Balthasar (1905–1988), I would not think it worth the trouble to argue, as he does, that—given the paradoxes and seemingly irreconcilable pronouncements of scriptures on the final state of all things—Christians *may* be allowed to *dare* to hope for the salvation of all. In fact, I have very small patience for this kind of "hopeful universalism," as it is often called. As far as I am concerned, anyone who hopes for the universal reconciliation of creatures with God must already believe that this would be the best possible ending to the Christian story; and such a person has then no excuse for imagining that God could bring any but the best possible ending to pass without thereby being in some sense a failed creator. The position I want to attempt to argue, therefore, to see how well it holds together, is far more extreme: to wit, that, if Christianity is in any way true, Christians dare not doubt the salvation of all, and that any understanding of what God accomplished in Christ that does not include the assurance of a final apokatastasis in which all things created are

---

8. MacDonald, *Evangelical Universalist*, 4.
9. Hart, *That All Shall Be Saved*, 66.

redeemed and joined to God is ultimately entirely incoherent and unworthy of rational faith.[10]

David Bentley Hart sees Christian universalism as the only Christianity worthy of coherent and rational faith, for anything short of the final salvation of all ultimately impinges on the absolute goodness of God. The mystery Hart deals with revolves around how it could be possible for creation to have anything other than a purely good end if it originates from a purely good beginning in a purely good God. The only logical conclusion of such a creation would be one in which the goodness of God finally permeates everyone and God is all in all. Thomas Talbott concurs with Hart on this matter writing, "I am prepared to endorse every major theological claim in [David Bentley Hart's *That All Shall be Saved*], starting with this one, which I take to be the main thesis of the book: 'if Christianity taken as a whole is indeed an entirely coherent and credible system of belief, then the universalist understanding of its message is *the only one possible*' (p.3—my emphasis)."[11]

The primary mystery the Inclusive/Christian universalist approach grapples with is this: how can God be all-good, all-knowing, and all-powerful and grace *not* save all? Those who take the Christian universalist viewpoint may have diverse opinions about exactly how necessary this approach is for Christianity to be credible, but they all agree that God can and will ultimately restore even the most recalcitrant of God's children.

Confidence in the Power of God to Restore

Christian universalists see restoration in store even for the hardest of cases. Consider the following two hard cases found in the New Testament: the apostle Paul and the Gerasene demoniac. We might not initially consider Paul to be a hard case. Yet Paul considered himself to be the hardest of hard cases, even the chief of sinners, because he led the opposition to Jesus' church. Paul's conversion account, found in the ninth chapter of Acts, demonstrates the power of Christ to dramatically change a person's perspective. Paul was on his way from Jerusalem to Damascus to round up followers of the Way (as the Jesus movement was initially called). Suddenly something like a flash bomb of blinding light went off. Paul fell to the ground, and

---

10. Hart, *That All Shall Be Saved*, 66.
11. Talbott, "Reviews 'That All Shall Be Saved.'"

then he heard a voice asking, "Why are you persecuting me?" Paul asked who was speaking to him. The voice identified itself as Jesus, and then commanded Paul to get up, go into the city of Damascus, and there be given instructions. When Paul got up he discovered he was blind. He was taken to Damascus, and for the next three days did not eat or drink anything. After that a follower of Jesus placed his hands on him and Paul's sight was restored. The next thing we know Paul is being baptized and starting to preach and evangelize. God had no trouble breaking through Paul's determined resistance. Once Paul literally saw the light, he was set free and he knew which direction he really wanted to go. Paul was resolute in his rejection of Christ. Yet his sensibilities changed drastically once he encountered the risen Christ on the road to Damascus.

The Gerasene demoniac is another illustrative hard case. Luke, in the eighth chapter of his gospel, tells about how Jesus and his disciples sailed across the Sea of Galilee to the region of the Gerasenes. There Jesus met a demon-possessed man known to history as the Gerasene demoniac. This man lived unclothed and unsheltered among the tombs. He'd become so crazed he'd been chained hand and foot and kept under guard. But even these precautions didn't keep him from getting loose and going out into lonely places. Jesus encounters the man, driving the unclean spirits out of him and into a herd of unclean animals (pigs) who rush down a steep bank into the lake and drown. Those who'd been herding the pigs went into town to tell what they'd seen. When the people of the town came out to see for themselves what had happened, they found the insane man to be "dressed and in his right mind" (Luke 8:35). What we can take note of here is that when the man was not in his right mind he was being driven to do things that went against his well-being. When he was not in his right mind he was bound—not free. But when Jesus broke the grip of evil and restored him to his right mind, then he was free. His freed will wanted nothing more than to be with Jesus.

No matter how hardened a child of God may become, they still retain their essential spiritual orientation towards God. Like Paul and the Gerasene demoniac, we too may resist God's initial saving efforts. We may even become convinced we don't want God and God doesn't want us. We may become so deeply attached to the lies and evil which inform our rebellion that we can't even imagine ever wanting to come home to God. Like the Gerasene demoniac, we might go out of our minds and become crazed. However, God can still break through. Our wills only become truly free once they are finally liberated from all falsehood and evil and sin. And once our wills become truly free there is only one direction they want to go—home.

Our Unalienable Right

We do not have a choice about being the children of a perfectly good God, and we cannot revoke our essence as God's child. But instead of thinking of this as a limitation of our free will, why not see our God-ward spiritual orientation as something which is our deepest right and privilege to express? I haven't met anyone born in the United States of America who considers it a burden to live in a country where our birthright includes certain rights—among those being life, liberty, and the pursuit of happiness. Our founders believed these rights were endowed by God to all, and that all were created equal. Since these rights were gifted by God to all people they could not be revoked by kings or governments. Because these universal human rights came directly from God, our founders considered them to be inalienable.

In a similar way, it is the inalienable right and privilege of each human being to be a child of God. Although this core identity may be marred, tarnished, and soiled, it cannot be revoked. The goodness of God, our heavenly Father, has been bestowed upon us at the deepest level of our beings. This is our original blessing. Early-church scholar Illaria Ramelli draws out the implications of this as being that "in the end there will be no more evil, and this is not incompatible with human freedom. Indeed, the eventual return of all to God will not cancel out human freedom of will, because human *orientation towards God* is part and parcel of human creatural nature."[12] As Ramelli points out, since children of God are inherently oriented towards God, once we have come to our senses, it would be a *violation* of our free will to keep us from returning home to God. Once we are truly free, we desire nothing more than the homecoming for which we were created.

True Freedom

And so, our freedom is connected with our identity. We are only truly free when we are being who we truly are—sons and daughters of the perfectly good and loving God. David Bentley Hart makes a helpful distinction along

---

12. Ramelli, *Christian Doctrine of Apokatastasis*, 820. Emphasis mine.

these lines when he argues for thinking of this as a higher understanding of human freedom. As Hart puts it,

> A higher understanding of human freedom . . . is inseparable from a definition of human nature. To be free is to be able to flourish as the kind of being one is, and so to attain the ontological good toward which one's nature is oriented; freedom is the unhindered realization of a complex nature in its proper end (natural and supernatural), and this is consummate liberty and happiness. The will that chooses poorly, then—through ignorance, maleficence, or corrupt desire—has not thereby become freer, but has further enslaved itself to those forces that prevent it from achieving its full expression.[13]

As Hart points out, we cannot think about being free apart from thinking about who we really and truly are. God grants us the ability to act in defiance of our true nature as God's children. However, each step we take in the wrong direction makes us less free and sets in motion the negative consequences which inevitably follow. There are real costs which stem from our sinful rebellions. Along these lines, Talbott remarks:

> Though our present choices cannot alter our final destiny, they most assuredly can affect our chances for happiness in the present and in the near-term future; and though our glorious inheritance cannot elude us forever, it most assuredly can elude us for a lifetime, or perhaps even for several lifetimes.
>
> So our choices do have very real consequences in our lives; indeed, these consequences are one of the means by which God will transform us in the end and thereby secure our final destiny. When we finally weary of our own selfishness, petty jealousies, and lust for power; when we learn at last, perhaps through bitter experience, that these lead only to ruin and cannot bring enduring happiness, that nothing short of union with God and reconciliation with others will satisfy our own deepest yearnings; when we discover that the Hound of Heaven has finally closed off every alternative to such a union, we shall then, each of us, finally embrace the destiny that is ours.[14]

As Talbott observes, it may take God a long time to finally defeat all of our delusions of will. But God is far more patient and intelligent than we are. God, our perfect heavenly parent, is like a grandmaster in chess when

13. Hart, *Doors of the Sea*, 71.
14. Talbott, *Inescapable Love of God*, 225.

it comes to playing against our deluded wills. Our deluded wills are allowed to make any move they wish, but God is also able to make the appropriate countermove. God will gradually and persistently hem in and finally defeat our deluded wills for our own good. The defeat of our deluded will results in the liberation of our true one. Once our true will comes forward we will find, perhaps to our great surprise, that we want nothing more than to come home. We think we know what we want—yet over the course of time, however much time it takes, we will begin to understand we only think we know what we want. And God, the persistent grandmaster, is always working in the background, laying the groundwork for the moment when our eyes are finally opened to the truth.[15]

God grants each of us a huge measure of liberty. In the course of our lifetimes we are all humbled by the reality of our inability to manage our liberty without getting off track. Some of us fall more seriously off track than others, but all of us fall off track to some degree. Some of us fall so far off track we lose the desire for the things of God. We bring great hardship on ourselves and on others. It may seem that some of us have become so ruined that even God can't restore us back to sanity. But the God for whom all things are possible can finally free us from all the lies and evil which bind us. Once we are finally liberated we will be truly free, and then we will want nothing more than to come back home.

God's Decisive Decision for Us

Noted theologian Jurgen Moltmann understands very well the tensions which arise when attempting to resolve the dilemma of God's sovereign will on the one hand and human self-will on the other. Yet he resolves these tensions with the insight that God's decision *for* us is stronger than any decision made *against* us, even our own. About the priority of God's decision on our behalf, Moltmann reasons:

> Who makes the decision about the salvation of lost men and women, and where is the decision made? Every Christian theologian is bound to answer: God decides for a person and for his or her

---

15. God, to quote Talbott again, is "like the grandmaster in chess who, though exercising no direct causal control over the moves of a novice, is nonetheless able to checkmate the novice in the end. Given an adequate analysis of freedom, moreover, we can even see why in the very nature of the case God cannot fail to win in the end" (Talbott, *Inescapable Love of God*, 170).

salvation, for otherwise there is no assurance of salvation at all. 'If God is for us, who can be against us . . .' (Rom. 8.31f.)—we may add: not even we ourselves! God is 'for us': that has been decided once and for all in the self-surrender and raising of Christ. It is not just a few of the elect who have been reconciled with God, but the whole cosmos (II Cor. 5.19). It is not just believers whom God loved, but the world (John 3.16). The great turning point from disaster to salvation took place on Golgotha; it does not just happen for the first time at the hour when we decide for faith, or are converted. Faith means experiencing and receiving this turning point personally, but faith is not the turning point itself. It is not my faith that creates salvation for me; salvation creates for me faith. If salvation and damnation were the results of human faith or unfaith, God would be dispensable. The connection between act and destiny, and the law of karma, would suffice to create the causal link. If, even where eternity is at stake, everyone were to forge their own happiness and dig their own graves, human beings would be their own God. It is only if a qualitative difference is made between God and human beings that God's decision and human decision can be valued and respected. God's decision 'for us', and our decisions for faith or disbelief no more belong on the same level than do eternity and time.[16]

All theologians have to find a way to resolve the tension between human liberty and divine sovereignty. Some theologians find themselves landing in a place of mystery, which prevents them from seeing through to whether or not God will finally be able to save all. The cautions recommended by the hopeful inclusivists are understandable. People are capricious, and they often make irrational decisions. However, we are not necessarily theologically hamstrung by these concerns. There is a very good case to be made that God's decision for us in Christ is ultimately greater than any foolish decision we can make against it.

George MacDonald (1824–1905), the famous Scottish minister, author, and poet, had a profound way of seeing through all of these mysteries to the final victory of God in the life of each person. Michael Phillips, an authority on MacDonald's theology, describes the way MacDonald anticipated the moment in which the light of God would finally break through the darkness of each and every rebellious soul:

> George MacDonald is known today as a "universalist," or believer in universal reconciliation, which holds that all souls will

16. Moltmann, *Coming of God*, 245.

ultimately be reconciled to God. While MacDonald never to my knowledge used those terms himself, he certainly believed that God would never abandon any of his creatures. In *The Last Farthing*, he paints a picture of what hell might be like, a grotesquely bleak vision of man alone with his own self, utterly bereft of the presence of God, which, unbeknownst to him, had been all that had ever made life bearable in the past. It is similar to the hell that C.S. Lewis imagines, in which the gates are locked from the inside; but where MacDonald differs is in his belief that such an existence *would be impossible for any man to abide*. At some point, the faintest glimmer of repentance would lighten the utter blackness of the prison of self. And so MacDonald imagines "a thousand steps up from the darkness, each a little less dark, a little nearer the light— but ah, the weary way! He cannot come out until he will have paid the uttermost farthing! Repentance once begun, however, may grow more and more rapid! If God once gets a willing hold, if with but one finger he touches the man's self, swift as possibility will he draw him from the darkness into the light.[17]

Christian universalists believe God's sovereignty and human freedom don't have to be tied up in a completely unresolvable mystery. We see how God can allow a tremendous amount of rebellion and still accomplish God's redemptive purposes. As humans we do have a choice. We can choose to resist God if we wish. However, God also has a choice—a choice more powerful than ours. God has the choice and the ability to break through even the hardest of wills and set them truly free.

Even though there are good reasons to believe God will finally save all in the end, there is still much hesitancy about adopting this as part of modern Christianity. This, however, was not the case in the early centuries of the church. And that's what we investigate next.

---

17. Phillips, "Introduction," Kindle location 124. Emphasis mine.

7

Authenticity

> Although no formal doctrine of hell existed in the early church, some of our ancient church fathers sought to correct ideas of eternal punishment with their interpretations of Scripture. Irenaeus, Origen, Clement of Alexandria, and Gregory of Nyssa strenuously and publically objected to notions of hell that depict God as an angry judge, waiting to throw the wicked into eternal torment for temporal sins.
>
> —Sharon Baker Putt[1]

Authentic Christianity and Everlasting Hell

Is AUTHENTIC CHRISTIANITY BOUND to an everlasting hell? Many assume so. Yet, in the earliest centuries of the Christian faith this was not the case. Substantial numbers of early Christians rejected the idea of eternal torment, and a number of early Christian leaders went on record as to their belief that God would ultimately save all. Robin Parry gives the following succinct historical overview:

> Christian universalism is . . . an ancient Christian theological position that in the early church stood alongside annihilation and eternal torment as a viable Christian opinion. The view is perhaps most closely associated with the great biblical scholar and pastoral theologian Origen (c. 184—c. 254), but precursors to his thought can be found in Bardaisan of Edessa (154—222) [and] Clement of Alexandria (c. 150—c. 215). . . . other names of note arguably include Theognostus (c. 210—c. 270), Pierius (†309), Gregory the Wonderworker (c. 213—c. 270), Pamphilus († 309), Methodius of

1. Putt, *Razing Hell*, xiii.

> Olympus († c. 311), Eusebius (c. 260—c. 340), Athanasius (296—373), Didymus the Blind († c. 398), Basil of Caesarea (c. 329—79), Gregory of Nyssa (c. 335—c. 395), Gregory of Nazianzen (c. 329—c. 390), Evagrius Pontocus (345—99), Diodore of Tarsus († c. 390), Theodore of Mopsuestia (c. 350—428), the younger Jerome (c. 347—420), Rufinus (c. 340—410), Dionysius the Areopagite (sixth century), Maximus the Confessor (c. 580—662), Isaac of Nineveh († 700), and John Scotus Eriugena (c. 815—c. 877).[2]

As Parry's list demonstrates, Christian universalism was a viable option which was well represented in early Christianity. Gregory of Nyssa is a standout among this group. He was a very important early church leader who helped define orthodoxy through his participation in forming the Nicene Creed (381). He was later named "Father of the Fathers" by the seventh general council of the church (787). Gregory clearly taught that the goodness of God would finally work through Christ to bring forgiveness and purification to all souls. Gregory believed that just as doctors sometimes cannot heal without causing pain, God is sometimes likewise forced to pursue a painful cure when there is no other option. Here are some of Gregory's own words on God's healing ways:

> For as those who scrape off calluses and warts contrary to nature which have become attached to the body with a knife or cautery do not apply to the one being treated a painless cure . . . so also whatever sort of material accretions are becoming callous on our souls which have become fleshly through fellowship with the passions are cut away and scraped off at the time of judgment by that indescribable wisdom and power of the one who, just as the Gospel says, "heals those who are sick." For it says, "those who are healthy have no need of a physician, but rather those who are sick."[3]

Gregory also compared God's purification of souls to the way metals are refined. He described the process this way:

> But as for those whose weaknesses have become inveterate . . . it is absolutely necessary that they should come to be in something proper to their case—just as the furnace is the proper thing for gold alloyed with dross—in order that, the vice which has been

---

2. Parry, "A Universalist View," 101–2.
3. Harmon, "Subjection of All Things," 59.

mixed up in them being melted away after long succeeding ages, their nature may be restored pure again to God.[4]

Gregory of Nyssa understood God to be the ultimate physician and purifier of souls. And he is an excellent example of a very influential early Christian who believed God would ultimately heal and purify everyone.

Tolerance in Early Christianity

In the early church there was a variety of opinions about final judgment. But the early Christians tolerated these differences of opinion. They didn't shy away from clearly stating their opposing views, but neither did they doubt the authenticity of each other's faith. Consider the example of Augustine (354–430), arguably the father of theology in the Western church. Augustine was for a time sympathetic to the idea that God would save all, but later in life he changed his mind, ultimately concluding that hell was best understood as never-ending torment.[5] Yet Augustine himself admitted that the vast majority—literally the *immo quam plurimi*—of his Christian contemporaries did not share his views about hell being eternal torment.[6] In the ancient world handbooks were called *enchiridions*. And in Augustine's handbook on the Christian faith, entitled *Enchiridion on Faith, Hope, and Love*, he wrote,

> It is quite in vain, then, that some—indeed very many—yield to merely human feelings and deplore the notion of the eternal punishment of the damned and their interminable and perpetual misery. They do not believe that such things will be. Not that they would go counter to divine Scripture—but, yielding to their own human feelings, they soften what seems harsh and give a milder emphasis to statements they believe are meant more to terrify than to express the literal truth. "God will not forget," they say, "to show mercy, nor in his anger will he shut up his mercy."[7]

Regarding this section from Augustine's *Enchiridion*, Thomas Talbott observes, " . . . this passage illustrates, the idea of universal reconciliation was very much a live option within the early church. For it was not

---

4. Sarris, *Heaven's Doors*, 51.
5. Ramelli, *Christian Doctrine of Apokatastasis*, 659.
6. Ramelli, *Christian Doctrine of Apokatastasis*, 672.
7. Augustine, *Enchiridion on Faith*, chapter 29, section 112, Kindle location 1803.

merely some, but 'very many,' who opposed the idea of eternal punishment, and these 'very many' were not pagans, but Christians, those with no desire to 'go counter to divine Scripture.'"[8] Augustine had a term he used for Christians who didn't believe in an eternal hell. He called them *misericordes*—meaning merciful ones. Illaria Ramelli notes that Augustine considered the *misericordes* to be "those merciful Christians who refuse to believe that infernal punishments will be *eternal*."[9] Augustine disagreed with these *misericordes*, but he recognized them as fellow Christians who were not intending to go counter to Scripture. However, as time went on in the Western church, the tolerance afforded to the *misericordes* would become smaller and smaller.

Imperial Christianity and Intolerance

In the history of Christianity in the Western world there is a noticeable difference between the tolerance of pre-imperial Christianity and the intolerance of post-imperial Christianity. Pre-imperial Christianity was a non-violent movement persecuted by the Roman Empire. It accommodated a variety of opinions with regard to how many would finally be saved. It was familiar with the nuances of the native Greek language in which the New Testament was written. It was able to include those who believed God was about the business of saving all people in Christ. It had no one view of hell or no one view of God's judgment to which every Christian was expected to adhere. Some of its leading figures were church fathers who believed all of God's judgments were ultimately purifying and restorative in nature.

But once the Roman Empire took on Christianity as a legitimate Roman religion, it increasingly began to use Christianity as it had always used religion. Religion was a tool of the state. Part of its purpose was to bring order and control. Religion, conquering, violence, and control all went together. Roman imperial Christianity translated the Bible into Latin, the language of the empire. The translation of the Bible into Latin contributed, along with other factors, to a harsher understanding of God's judgments within the Western church. Instead of having a Hebrew or Greek view of time moving forward in coming ages or *aions*, the Roman imperial church had a Latin view of a static future. They anticipated eternal states, from the Latin word *aeternum*, either of glory or of torment. In imperial Christianity

8. Talbott, *Inescapable Love of God*, 16.
9. Ramelli, *Christian Doctrine of Apokatastasis*, 672.

it became understood that all who were in the church were headed for an *aeternum* of bliss, while all outside of it were headed for an *aeternum* of *iusti*. From the Latin word *iusti* comes the English word "justice." The damned were in for an eternity of justice. God's justice, in order to be satisfied, required an eternity of torment. The imperial church did not think in Greek about God's judgment being a restorative, purifying process which would take place in coming ages. Instead, it thought in Latin about God's judgment being a retributive, tormenting process which lasted for all eternity. This harsh Latin theology became orthodoxy. Augustine, the primary theologian of the Latin-speaking Western church, could not read Greek and disliked the language. His inability to read the New Testament in its original language affected his ability to interpret it. Augustine's harsh, Latin theology ended up overshadowing the gentle and forgiving theology of the Greek-speaking early church fathers.

In the first several hundred years of imperial Christianity it was the emperor himself who was the head of the church. Perhaps no other Roman emperor better embodied the desire to unite the power of the state with Christianity than the emperor Justinian. In Justinian's Christian empire Jews were persecuted and pagans lost their rights to teach their beliefs. Justinian wanted one unified version of the Christian faith in his empire, and he wielded his power towards accomplishing this goal.

The Controversy Surrounding Origen

One of the doctrinal disputes Justinian became involved in had to do with certain beliefs which had grown out of some of Origen's ideas. Origen (184–254) was one of the most prominent early church fathers to support the universal restoration of all souls back to God. Origen was speculative and wide-ranging in his thinking, but during his day the boundaries of Christian thought were not as firmly instituted as they would later become. After Origen's time some took his ideas even further in ways he himself would likely have not anticipated. The emperor Justinian believed that Origen, and those who further developed his ideas, should be condemned. The Italian patristics scholar Ilaria Ramelli, in her book on the early history of Christian universalism, includes an extensive account of the confusing situation surrounding the condemnation of Origen. She then summarizes her conclusions this way:

The so-called "condemnation of Origen" by "the Church" in the sixth century probably never occurred proper, and even if it occurred it did so only as a result of a long series of misunderstandings, when the anthropological, eschatological, and psychological questions were no longer felt as open to investigation—as Origen ... considered them—but dogmatically established.

The aforementioned condemnation was in fact a condemnation, not at all of Origen, but rather of a late and exasperated form of Origenism; moreover, it was mainly wanted by emperor Justinian—or better his counselors, given that he was not a theologian—and only partially, or even not at all, ratified by ecclesiastical representatives.[10]

The fifth general church council (553), which is associated with the supposed condemnation of Origen, was full of confusion and misunderstanding. Scholars today debate the many perplexing details of what happened before and after that council. The reason for all the confusion is that by that time the name of Origen became tangled up with all kinds of speculative ideas which went beyond the basic proposition that God would ultimately save all. As Parry notes:

> In the three hundred years between [Origen's] death and the fifth ecumenical council his ideas had been picked up and developed in more radical directions than one finds in Origen's own work. Indeed, arguably, Origen himself would have agreed with some of these anathemas. In part it was the theology of these Origenists—people such as Evagrius of Pontus (346–399), rather than that of Origen himself, that was condemned by Justinian and the council. But neither the council nor the later church made this distinction between Origen and Origenism—he was the seed from which the plant had grown, even if it had mutated as it developed—and thus he was condemned, in part, for the theological views of his heirs.[11]

Phillip Schaff, editor of *The Complete Works of the Church Fathers*, describes the unusual way in which the emperor Justinian convened the council:

> It must be admitted that before the opening of the council, which had been delayed by the resistance of the pope, the bishops already assembled at Constantinople had to consider, by order of the emperor, a form of Origenism that had practically nothing in

---

10. Ramelli, *Christian Doctrine of Apokatastasis*, 724–25.
11. MacDonald, *"All Shall Be Well,"* 7.

common with Origen, but which was held, we know, by one of the Origenist parties in Palestine ... The bishops certainly subscribed to the fifteen anathemas proposed by the emperor ... but there is no proof that the approbation of the pope, who was at that time protesting against the convocation of the council, was asked. It is easy to understand how this extra-conciliary sentence was mistaken at a later period for a decree of the actual ecumenical council.[12]

The results of the fifth ecumenical council are definitive for Catholic and Orthodox Christians. However, given the many problems with this council, there are those among the Catholic and the Orthodox that do not consider the ultimate restoration of humanity to have ever been anathematized or pronounced heretical. Orthodox theologian David Bentley Hart gives the following bracing assessment of the fifth general council:

> [It] is the most shameful episode in the history of Christian doctrine. For one thing, to have declared any man a heretic three centuries after dying in the peace of the Church, in respect of doctrinal determinations not reached during his life, was a gross violation of all legitimate canonical order; but in Origen's case it was especially loathsome. After Paul, there is no single Christian figure to whom the whole tradition is more indebted. It was Origen who taught the Church how to read Scripture as a living mirror of Christ, who evolved the principles of later trinitarian theology and Christology, who majestically set the standard for Christian apologetics, who produced the first and richest expositions of contemplative spirituality, and who—simply said—laid the foundation of the whole edifice of developed Christian thought. Moreover, he was not only a man of extraordinary personal holiness, piety, and charity, but a martyr as well: Brutally tortured during the Decian persecution at the age of sixty-six, he never recovered, but slowly withered away over a period of three years.
>
> I cannot really say what irks me more, though: that it happened or that, in fact, it really never did. The oldest records of the council ... make it clear that those fifteen anathemas were never even discussed by the assembled bishops, let alone ratified, published, or promulgated. And since the late nineteenth century various scholars have convincingly established that neither Origen nor "Origenism" was ever the subject of any condemnation pronounced by the "holy fathers" in 553. The best modern critical

---

12. Schaff, *Complete Works*, under "Second Origenistic Crisis" in "Origenist Controversies," Kindle location 493005.

edition of the Seven Councils—Norman Tanner's—simply omits the anathemas as spurious interpolations.[13]

Catholic priest, and noted authority on spiritual formation, Richard Rohr is also of the opinion that the ultimate restoration of humanity was never officially condemned by the church. As Rohr sees it,

> There were a number of fathers in the early church (the first four centuries) who believed in apokatastasis, which means "universal restoration" (Acts 3:21). They believed that the real meaning of the resurrection of Christ was that God's love was so perfect and so victorious that in fact it would finally win out in every single person's life. . . . When I read the history of the church and its dogma, I see apokatastasis was never condemned as heretical. We may believe it if we want to. We were never told we had to believe it, but neither was it condemned . . . We almost hold out for universal restoration: that the true meaning of the raising of Jesus is that God will turn all our human crucifixions into resurrection. . . .
>
> Could God's love really be that great and that universal? Is life just a great school of love? I believe it is. Love is the lesson, and God's love is so great that God will finally teach it to all of us. We'll finally surrender, and God will finally win. That will be God's "justice."[14]

The hope of an ultimate restoration of humanity is a magnificent and consummately consoling thought. Unfortunately, this profoundly consoling and hopeful thought was almost completely removed from the Christian imagination in Western civilization. The hope of a full human restoration was mainly restricted to those who had access to theological education and church history. And even then, the controversy surrounding Origen in the sixth century led to a lasting cloud over the proposition that God would eventually deliver all from the grip of sin and death. As the church continued through its history, these and other doctrinal controversies intensified. Increasing doctrinal disagreements, combined with the alliance of church and state, led to much violence being done in the name of Christ. And, underneath it all, further stoking the flames of these conflicts, would be the doctrine of a never-ending hell.

---

13. Hart, "Saint Origen."
14. Rohr, *Everything Belongs*, 132–33.

Christian Violence and the Doctrine of Eternal Torment

From the time of the middle ages forward, doctrinal disputes would continue to plague Christianity and ultimately lead to violence in the cause of protecting Christian orthodoxy as it was then understood. The Protestant Reformation would result in even more violence between Christians over doctrine. No doubt there were many political and financial motives at play in all of this, but one of the reasons Christianity became so violent in the history of Western civilization was because it had come to believe in a God who tortured God's enemies forever in hell. These violent Christians were merely imitating the violent God of their understanding. It only made sense to them to kill heretics, who were far more dangerous than murderers. A murderer could only kill the body, but a heretic could lead a soul to eternal damnation. Along these lines, Talbott observes:

> Religious persecution in the Western church typically has had its roots in an obsessive fear of eternal damnation. It is no doubt possible to believe in eternal damnation without believing that God would be so unjust as to damn someone eternally for an honest mistake in abstract theology. But fear is often irrational, and, as a matter of historical fact, the organized Christian church has consistently employed the fear of eternal damnation as a weapon against supposed theological error (as determined by self-appointed authorities, of course). It has consistently cultivated in its constituency the fear that those who die in unbelief, or with certain mistaken beliefs, are precisely those whom God will damn eternally in hell. Such fear, which springs ultimately from a lack of confidence (or faith) in the character of God, has had disastrous consequences in the life of the church. Having no confidence in the love of God, those in the grips of such fear have too often wielded the sword in a sincere effort to protect their loved ones from the tragic consequences, as they have seen it, of error in religious matters.[15]

This historical chain of events explains why the early, diverse, non-violent, optimistic, Greek-language-based version of Christianity was largely forgotten in Western civilization. Thankfully, we are now free once again to consider the optimistic theology of early church fathers such as Gregory of Nyssa. The last few hundred years has generated much scholarship on these issues. And with the advent of the internet, the general public is no

---

15. Talbott, *Inescapable Love of God*, 26–27.

longer barred from accessing this information. Because of this resurgence of awareness, the early optimistic version of Christianity is being remembered and revived today. And, in many cases, the most enthusiastic revival of the early hopeful view is being led by Christians with backgrounds in the evangelical wing of the Christian faith.

Evangelicals and Christian Universalism

One sign pointing to a revival of the Inclusive/Christian universalist approach among Evangelicals can be seen in the way Zondervan Publishing reissued one of its books on the topic of hell. In Zondervan's first edition of *Four Views on Hell* (released in 1996) there was no recognition that evangelical Christians could even consider an Inclusive/Christian universalist approach to hell. But things changed so much in the twenty years since the first edition of the book that a new edition, one which included a Christian universalist perspective, was in order. Preston Sprinkle, editor of the new edition, makes the following observation in the introduction: "Christian universalism is gaining ground. . . . While some proponents of universalism—the belief that everyone will eventually be rescued out of hell—base their view on sentimentality, others are digging it out of the biblical narrative. As you will see in the following pages, there are some powerful biblical arguments that Christians need to wrestle with. No longer can evangelicals scoff at this view as the byproduct of too many hours of Oprah."[16]

In this up-to-date second edition of *Four Views on Hell* Robin Parry contributes a chapter on Christian universalism and hell. At the end of the book, Preston Sprinkle, from his vantage point as the book's editor, makes the following comment in the book's conclusion:

> I found Robin Parry's essay to be a fascinating read! And, if I can be quite honest, I think it is a game-changer. I do not say this because I agree with his ultimate conclusion (I don't), but because he has brought what is often assumed to be a heretical view into the arena of biblical exegesis and theology. Christians can no longer dismiss his view as *unorthodox*. We must now actually crack open our Bibles and, like the noble Bereans (Acts 17:11), see if these things are so. . . . Evangelicals must think deeply and critically—indeed,

---

16. Sprinkle, *Four Views on Hell*, 10.

biblically—about Parry's argument. And if I can be completely honest, I hope that Parry is right.[17]

Sprinkle, even though he disagrees with Parry, categorizes Parry's theology as an orthodox option for Christian belief. Sprinkle's assertion that Christian universalism is an orthodox option for Christian belief is very significant. I could never have imagined this kind evangelical openness back in 1996 when I consulted the first edition of *Four Views on Hell* as part of my Doctor of Ministry thesis. Back then I could not have guessed that twenty years later a second edition of this same book would be released in which a Christian universalist approach was deemed an orthodox option for Christian belief.

For Evangelicals who've been ostracized for believing God will save all, this can be life changing. George Sarris is a good example of one of these kinds of persons. Sarris is an Evangelical who believes in the inerrancy of Scripture. In preparation for ministry in the media world, he received education in an evangelical seminary. During his seminary training he began to investigate the idea that hell might not be God's last word for people. Sarris wrote a seminary paper on the topic. The professor gave him a good grade for the research he'd done, but then discouraged him about sharing his conclusions. However, over the years Sarris could not drop the idea. In 2017 he published his conclusions in his book *Heaven's Doors: Wider Than You Ever Believed!* On April 7, 2016, in Sarris's blog *Engaging the Culture*, he posted the following words. They are in a post entitled "A Game-Changer On Hell?" which reads in part:

> Until now, most Christians have assumed that evangelicals—people who base their convictions clearly on the teaching of Scripture—cannot possibly be universalists—people who believe that God will one day redeem all mankind. With the release on March 8 of Zondervan's *Four Views on Hell (Second Edition)*, that understanding suddenly changed! For the first time, a well-respected, evangelical publishing house has clearly acknowledged that universalism is a view Christians should seriously consider. . . .
>
> *Four Views on Hell (Second Edition)* is a great introduction to the Biblical arguments that directly relate to these issues. The arguments presented are not exhaustive. But they're clear and clearly presented. After reading Parry's essay, you still may not be convinced that he is right. But it's no longer enough to simply state categorically that an evangelical can't be a universalist! . . . The

---

17. Sprinkle, *Four Views on Hell*, 197–98. Emphasis mine.

landscape has changed. Maybe it's time to take another look at an issue you may have been wondering about for a very long time.[18]

Sarris describes Evangelicals as people who base their convictions clearly on the teaching of Scripture. For Evangelicals like Sarris, coming to believe God will ultimately save all is not a denial of Scripture but an affirmation of it. Evangelicals come out of the Protestant Reformation which had *sola scriptura* (Scripture alone) as one of its mottos. Sarris did not give up *sola scriptura* in reaching his conclusions—just the opposite. It was his attention to Scripture alone in its original languages and contexts, combined with his refusal to be intimidated by the pronouncements of debatable medieval church councils, which led him to his conclusions. Now Sarris, and others like him, can feel vindicated in that Zondervan, a major evangelical publishing house, has published a book which declares his point of view to be an orthodox option worthy of consideration.

Other Evangelicals are also recognizing a shift in thinking among their circles regarding Christian universalism. Roger Olson, a theologian on the faculty of the Baptist seminary at Baylor University in Waco, TX, is a good example of this. Olson, a professor of theology in an evangelical seminary, does not subscribe to an Inclusive/Christian universalist approach. But he is in a position to notice that there is much new thinking taking place about the possibility of it. Olson wrote in January 2015 that he can now envision, "[a] new stage among evangelicals where one can see a possible horizon in which universalism will be accepted as normal (but not normative) for evangelicals. In other words, an evangelical theologian who 'comes out of the closet' as embracing absolute universalism will not automatically be excommunicated from the evangelical movement by its popes."[19] Olson also stated in the same blog post, "One thing is becoming undeniably clear—to anyone who reads a broad spectrum of contemporary evangelical theology: universalism is 'in the air.' I mean it is being much discussed by evangelicals and not always only in negative ways. Many evangelicals are considering various options in universalism in a way that evangelicals in the past would not have done."[20]

Although Olson himself is not persuaded that God's grace will save all, he recognizes that some Evangelicals are beginning to have serious conversations about the possibility. Given that Christian universalism was a view

18. Sarris, "Game-Changer on Hell?"
19. Olson, "Universalism Is 'in the Air.'"
20. Olson, "Universalism Is 'in the Air.'"

held in the early days of Christianity, and that it is starting to be more vigorously remembered and defended as an orthodox possibility for Christians today, perhaps we are at a turning point. There is growing awareness that there is legitimate room within the Christian faith to believe Jesus reveals to us a God who will persist, even in judgment and hell if necessary, until all of us are saved and brought into one complete and joyful harmony.

Evangelical Push-Back

Even though there are some signs of evangelical openness to Christian universalism, there is still considerable opposition to it as well. A culmination of this opposition is found in Michael McClymond's two-volume work *The Devil's Redemption*. The title of McClymond's book is a reference to how universalism has led some to a believe not only in the ultimate restoration of all fallen humanity, but also of all created beings, including fallen angels and even the devil himself. McClymond, an evangelical scholar of Christian history, is concerned that Christian universalism, if allowed to go mainstream, will ultimately result in a weakening, and even a possible disintegration, of key Christian beliefs. Along these lines, he writes:

> The issue of final salvation for all, or final salvation for some, does not stand alone but is intertwined with virtually everything that Christianity has to say about God's love and justice, human nature, sin, freedom, Jesus' life, Jesus' death on the cross, Jesus' resurrection, the Holy Spirit, the nature of the church, and Jesus' return. For the same reason, a Christian affirmation of final, universal inclusion will affect everything else that one might say about God, humanity, Christ, sin, grace, salvation, and the church. . . . How much, theologically speaking, is at stake in the debate on universalism? The answer is: *everything*.[21]

McClymond represents Evangelicals who believe Christian universalism introduces a threat to the core of the Christian faith, and therefore it should be strongly refuted. While some within Evangelicalism may be warming to the possibility of an orthodox Christian universalism, others are taking a definite stand against it. At issue is what is actually central to the Christian faith versus what is peripheral. For Evangelicals, the gospel message has traditionally revolved around deliverance from some form of

---

21. McClymond, *Devil's Redemption*, xxiii–xxiv.

eternal hell. Therefore, anything that threatens the reality of an eternal hell threatens something that is central to their gospel message.

However, deliverance from an eternal hell is not the only way the gospel can be announced. It is quite possible to powerfully announce Jesus' good news about the kingdom of God, and to speak urgently about the dangers of God's judgment on sin, all without necessitating a belief in the eternality of hell. And, although many churches require belief in a hell-of-no-return for some number of people, it would be a great shame for spiritual seekers after Christ to be denied *all* church membership and Christian fellowship simply because they can't go along with such an understanding of God's judgment. And this leads me to a practical reason for modern Christianity to return to its earliest roots and to be more tolerant of Christian universalism.

A Practical Reason

There is a very practical reason for Christian universalism to be more widely recognized as a legitimate Christian option. More people would be able to experience the benefit of having a Jesus-centered spiritualty if they knew the Inclusive/Christian universalist approach was an option. But, not knowing this, they opt out of anything Christian because they assume being Christian requires believing in some form of never-ending hell. This is one of the main reasons they see Christianity as a harsh religion. Phillip Yancey, a popular evangelical Christian author, in his book *Vanishing Grace*, writes about how more and more young people are having a negative impression of Christianity, especially Evangelical Christianity. Yancey is not a Christian universalist, but he is an example of an evangelical Christian who clearly sees there is a problem. At the beginning of his book Yancey writes:

> I decided to write this book after I saw the results of surveys by the George Barna group. A few telling statistics jumped off the page. In 1996, 85 percent of Americans who had no religious commitment still viewed Christianity favorably. Thirteen years later, in 2009, only 16 percent of young "outsiders" had a favorable impression of Christianity, and just 3 percent had a good impression of evangelicals. I wanted to explore what caused that dramatic plunge in such a relatively short time. Why do Christians stir up hostile feelings—and what, if anything, should we do about it?[22]

22. Yancey, *Vanishing Grace*, 15.

Yancey also notes in his book the phenomenon of the "nones." The nones are those who, when polled about religious preference, respond by checking "none." Yancey observes, "Surveys show a steady rise in the 'nones' (now one-third of those under the age of thirty), that is, those who claim no religion, a category now larger than all Episcopalians, Presbyterians, Methodists, and Lutherans combined."[23] These people aren't necessarily anti-spiritual, but they are increasingly hesitant to be associated with institutional spirituality, i.e., churches.

Yancey isn't the only one who is concerned about this large-scale rejection of Christianity among the young. The same phenomenon is occurring in Europe as well. Richard Rohr, a Catholic priest who has published extensively on Christian spiritual formation, believes the eternal hell doctrine is part of the reason for this large-scale rejection of Christianity. Rohr believes the popular conception of Christianity as a religion which requires its adherents to believe in a God who torments or terminates spiritual failures in a hell-of-no-return has resulted in what he dramatically calls a culture that hates its religion.[24] Rohr puts it like this, "No culture can survive if it hates its religion. And that's where we're at right now."[25] Rohr argues the case that Christianity in America and Europe is viewed "to an amazing degree [with] a distrust, a dislike, a cynicism, and a desire to reject."[26]

In the midst of all of this rejection of the Christian faith why would Christians, at this crucial moment, want to hold up the doctrine of a never-ending hell of torment or of annihilation as a necessary part of being Christian? Why would we present Christianity as if escape from unending torment or final termination is a necessary part of any valid understanding of our faith? Why would we want to make people feel being Christian means having not only to accept Jesus as their savior, but also to accept that God either cannot or will not save everyone? When someone is becoming Christian must they first be asked, "Do you accept Jesus as your lord and savior, and do you deny God will ultimately save all?" What's wrong with letting people know one way of being Christian is to believe God is in the process of saving everyone by grace? Why is it Christians sing about an amazing grace which "saves a wretch like me" but then become troubled by the suggestion God will save all wretches by grace?

23. Yancey, *Vanishing Grace*, 15.
24. Rohr, "Hell, No!"
25. Rohr, "Hell, No!"
26. Rohr, "Hell, No!"

And so, on a very practical level, letting people know about the Inclusive/Christian universalist approach can open the doors of Christian faith and Christian community to many more people. In so doing we would not be doing something new, but returning to how it was in the early centuries of the Christian faith when this view was known and accepted. But there is an even more urgent concern to contend with, and it has to do with the goodness of God.

Upholding the Goodness of God

The final, and perhaps most important, reason for advocating the Inclusive/Christian universalist approach has to do with upholding the goodness of God. Both the Transactional and Exclusive approaches to the faith each ask us to believe in a God who is good and yet who is knowingly the origin of people who inevitably come to tragic destinies—either of annihilation or eternal torment. How is it possible to square a God who is supposedly all-knowing, all-powerful, and all-good with outcomes which are not good for all? The Transactional/Arminian approach and the Exclusive/Calvinist approach, for all of their differences, generate the exact same problems in this regard. This is easier to see in the Exclusive approach where God does not even sincerely desire the salvation of all, which seems callous to say the least. But the same problem inevitably arises in the Transactional approach as well, and its appeal to free will doesn't solve the problem. For even if people only come to bad ends because of their own delusional choices, an all-knowing God still incurs moral responsibility through knowing about their tragic destiny in advance.

David Bentley Hart makes this problem plain and unavoidable. The core of Hart's argument is that since God is completely responsible for creation, God is also morally defined by it. Since God knows the end of creation from the beginning, then the outcome of creation becomes the final revelation of the character of God. And if there is any permanent evil in God's creation then the first cause of that evil is God, who knew it would inevitably occur from the beginning. And this means, as Hart succinctly ties it together, "that the moral destiny of creation and the moral nature of God are inseparable."[27]

This conclusion is hard to evade, because if God knows all outcomes from the beginning, then God ordains, in one way or another, all of those

27. Hart, *That All Shall Be Saved*, 69.

outcomes. Even if we choose to commit evil, that evil is still a known and anticipated consequence of creation. This makes God ultimately responsible for this evil, and so places the burden upon God to repair it as part of a larger redemptive plan for each person individually and for all persons corporately. All of this raises the question: How can God be thoroughly good if God creates, even indirectly, eternal outcomes which are not thoroughly good? Hart drives this observation home with his typical unflinching clarity:

> Because we say God creates freely, we must believe his final judgment shall reveal him for who he is. So, if all are not saved, if God creates souls he knows to be destined to eternal misery, is God evil? Well, why debate semantics. Maybe every analogy fails. What is not debatable is that, if God does so create, in himself he cannot be good as such. . . .
>
> We are presented by what has become the majority [Christian] tradition with three fundamental claims, any two of which might be true simultaneously, but never all three: that God freely created all things out of nothingness; that God is the Good itself; and it is certain or at least possible that some rational creatures will endure eternal loss of God. And this, I have to say, is the final moral meaning I find in the doctrine of *creatio ex nihilo*, at least if we truly believe that our language about God's goodness and the theological grammar to which it belongs are not empty, that the God of eternal retribution and pure sovereignty proclaimed by so much of the Christian tradition is not, and cannot possibly be, the God of self-outpouring love revealed in Christ. If God is the good creator of all, he is the savior of all, without fail, who brings to himself all he has made. . . . If he is not the savior of all, the Kingdom is only a dream, and creation something considerably worse than a nightmare. But, again, it is not so. God saw that it was good; and in the ages, we shall see it too.[28]

The reason this argument is so challenging is because it is rooted in the utter goodness of God. It is this very utter goodness of God which is at stake in any Christian tradition which asks us to believe in a God who is good while at the same time ascribing to this same God outcomes which are anything but good. For if God is the author of things which are not good in the ultimate sense, then God cannot be considered to be good in the ultimate sense. And the problem extends even to hopeful inclusivism. Even though hopeful inclusivism is hopeful, even confidently expectant,

---

28. Hart, *Hidden and the Manifest*, 358. An updated version of this essay is also present in Hart's *That All Shall be Saved*.

that all will be saved, it still allows for the possibility that all will not be saved. As David Bentley Hart points out, the same challenge to God's goodness arises even when it is "*at least possible* that some rational creatures will endure eternal loss of God."[29] If God puts us in a situation in which our ultimate loss is even possible, then God is answerable for this, even if none are finally lost. I refer to Hart again, who puts it more sharply: "But let us say God created simply *on the chance* that humanity might sin, and that a certain number of incorrigibly wicked souls might plunge themselves into Tartarus forever; this still means that, morally, he has purchased the revelation of his power in creation by the same horrendous price—even if, in the end no one at all happens to be damned."[30]

Possible threats to God's goodness arise even on the chance of God's creation resulting in some type of irreparable harm. Therefore, a convinced and unreserved Inclusive/Christian universalist approach is required in order to completely safeguard the goodness of God. This strong form of Christian universalism does not allow anything to possibly subtract from God's goodness. Every evil which is allowed is eventually turned back towards the good. The goodness of God, which reigned in the beginning, completely prevails in the end—and grace saves all.

---

29. Hart, *Hidden and the Manifest*, 350. Emphasis mine.
30. Hart, *Hidden and the Manifest*, 347.

8

My Story

> When we are lost in the woods the sight of a signpost is a great matter. He who first sees it cries "Look!" The whole party gathers round and stares. But when we have found the road and are passing signposts every few miles, we shall not stop and stare. They will encourage us and we shall be grateful to the authority that set them up.
>
> —C. S. Lewis[1]

As I look back over my life now I can see a clear set of spiritual signposts along the way. But it wasn't that way from the beginning. I didn't start out with any set ideas about spirituality. My parents were each raised in church, but, for various reasons, weren't attending church when I was growing up. They were both from Tennessee, but I grew up in Irving, Texas, where we'd moved for my father to pursue a career in commercial aviation after nine years in the air force. My mom devoted her time to the home and to me, the only child. When I was in second grade my mother, believing I should know something about Christianity, took me to visit a church of the kind the she'd attended as a child. That day the minister told a story about teenagers who'd gotten drunk, died in a car crash, and were sent to hell forever because they weren't saved (meaning they hadn't personally accepted Jesus into their hearts as Lord and Savior). After the church service I told mother, "That place is scary and I don't want to go back." Mother honored my request.

A few years later, when I was in the fifth grade, my parents arranged for a babysitter while they were out for the evening. Believing I was no longer a baby, I was not too excited by the whole affair. But when the

---

1. Lewis, *Surprised by Joy*, 290.

babysitter turned out to be a beautiful sixteen-year-old, I began to look forward to the evening. Little did I realize what was in store; for this young woman was very evangelical, and very armed with the gospel for my salvation. I'm sure she was just passing on to me what she had been taught. But she had been taught some pretty bracing things. She explained to me that even if I couldn't think of anything really bad I'd ever done, I was still a sinner, because everyone's a sinner, because everyone's born that way. And God, being holy, had to send sinners to hell forever unless they accepted Jesus into their hearts as Lord and Savior before they died. So, there I was, stuck in an odd situation: trapped by a beautiful messenger of a terrifying gospel. I did what any frightened kid might do in my situation. I caved. At her prompting, I followed along in a prayer where I invited Jesus into my heart. The experience just left me feeling even more vulnerable, confused, and terrified about God.

During my teenage years I had a few more church experiences, and they just reinforced my views about Christianity. God was going to send all of us teenagers to hell forever, and everyone else too, unless we believed and were saved. It seemed to me that church, and Christianity by extension, was all about avoiding eternal torment in hell. The church services I visited at the invitation of friends were all very emotional, with people crying and going up to the front to get saved at the end. But the emotion never seemed to hit me—just the opposite. The more emotional they all got, the more detached I became.

After high school I attended college at Texas Tech University in Lubbock, Texas. When I came back home for Christmas break, my mother had to tell me she and my father were getting divorced. My parent's divorce wasn't a mean, terrible affair. But for me it was still bracing. What bothered me was not just that my parents had divorced, but that several of my friends' parents had divorced as well. There seemed to be a pattern. The future was apparently a place of disillusionment where adults became disenchanted with their lives, their jobs, and their marriages. And then, when I peered out into the distant future, there waiting for me was the specter of aging and death. Even if I ever did happen to have a happy, satisfying life, eventually aging and death would take it all away from me. The more I thought about all of this the more depressed it made me. The idea of God didn't do much to help me. The angry Christian God to which I'd been introduced didn't give me much hope.

The summer after my first year at Texas Tech I came back home to Irving. I was exercising one day at a YMCA. Also working out at "the Y" that day was the youth minister of a hell-preaching church I'd visited at the urging of friends during high school. He noticed me and invited me to come by his office at the church. I was initially a little hesitant, but I accepted his invitation. So, I went by his office and told him about my reservations regarding Christianity. He listened and he didn't argue with me. He just recommended I might try reading C. S. Lewis's book *Mere Christianity*.

The Christianity C. S. Lewis described in *Mere Christianity* was quite a bit different from what I'd heard at the hell-preaching church. Lewis (1898–1963) had been a skeptic through a large part of his life, and I could really identify with his skepticism. But in *Mere Christianity* he laid out a reasonable, orderly account of his journey into faith. I didn't realize Christianity could be so logical and thoughtful. In this way C. S. Lewis became for me the first major signpost in my journey into the Christian faith.

Lewis himself was a highly educated British man, a professor of literature who taught at Cambridge and Oxford. Lewis also expressed his theological ideas through imaginative fiction. In his book *The Great Divorce* he told a whimsical story of a traveler taking a bus trip from the edges of hell to the borderlands of heaven, where any citizen of hell could become a citizen of heaven if they could just let go of the evil which was holding them back. On heaven's borderlands the traveler meets a wise old sage by the name of George MacDonald who explains how all spiritual travelers ultimately find what they truly seek. (I would discover later in life that George MacDonald, whom Lewis considered his spiritual mentor, was an actual person, a minister and author from Scotland who believed all the judgments of God—even hell itself—were ultimately restorative in nature.) I went on to read the *The Lion the Witch and the Wardrobe* and *The Last Battle*, the first and last books of Lewis's series The Chronicles of Narnia.

In *The Last Battle* there is a showdown between the forces of evil (led by the four-armed, vulture-headed Tash), and the forces of good (led by the great, talking lion, Aslan). Aslan, a Christ figure, ultimately wins the great battle. After the final battle there's a scene between Aslan and one of Tash's soldiers, named Emeth, who expects to be judged and destroyed by Aslan. Unexpectedly, Alsan shows Emeth grace and forgiveness instead, explaining how all true service, no matter how mistaken, ultimately counts as service to him.

In the writings of C. S. Lewis I discovered a Christian vision of a very good God, and I came to a true moment of faith. One day while praying I experienced the presence of God and intense waves of peace and joy and hope. Back at Texas Tech I tried different churches. On the recommendation of friend who knew my story, I visited and joined First Christian Church, a congregation of the Christian Church (Disciples of Christ). This church, as I experienced it, wasn't a hell-preaching church, but a love-preaching church. This church put no limits on the love of God and encouraged each member to come to their own best interpretation of the Bible as they followed Jesus as Lord and Savior. Ultimately this church encouraged and sponsored my seminary education and I entered the ministry.

In 2005 I started really focusing my ministry on spiritual growth. I began to realize that unless someone truly caught on to the genuine joy of ongoing spiritual growth, the experience of church would eventually burn them out. If church was the only place people were experiencing spirituality, then sooner or later the challenges and frustrations of church would overwhelm the benefits, and they would drift off. But if church was part of a true excitement about the daily experience of spiritual growth then both the frustrations and rewards of church would be able to fit into their spiritual lives in the right way. I wondered what motivation there could be which would be pure enough to empower such excitement about spiritual growth. The only sufficiently powerful motivation I could see would be the development of a true desire for an ever-increasing experience of the perfect love at the heart of God. It seemed to me spiritual growth would flounder if its purpose was either to earn salvation or to earn God's love. I came to believe that if spiritual growth was really going to last for the long term it had to be driven by something extremely positive and powerful. The only engine I could see which qualified was a deep desire to experience everything good at the heart of a truly good God.

But then this led me to some hard questions: How much certainty do we actually have that God's goodness has really got us? Is there a point at which God's goodness towards us runs out and God gives up? Is there a point of failure God lets us get past where we are lost to God forever? Also during this time I was in a theological discussion group with some church members. Our discussions revolved around the topics of eternal destinies and the purpose of God's judgments. A couple of the members of the group encouraged me to rethink my negative position on Christian universalism. I had considered it before, but I wasn't quite convinced. I was concerned that

Christian universalism violated free will. It seemed to me, at the time, while God wanted to save all people, some people may embrace evil to such an extent that they'd eventually become completely overtaken by it. Also, my impression at the time was that most universalists were not really orthodox Christians, but rather spiritual pluralists who believed all roads equally led to heaven. However, I was, and still am, of the opinion that any path which leads to heaven has to eventually go through Christ.

Then came a very significant meeting. I was having lunch one day with a member of the discussion group. He had come to embrace Christian universalism, and he pointedly said to me, "I would never give up on any of my children—ever. And I don't see how I'm a better parent than God." My wife and I weren't able to have children so I've never experienced the depth of feeling for a child my friend was talking about. I began to wonder if never being a father might have caused a blind spot in my own theology. I resolved to catch up on what had been written on the topic of Christian universalism since I had studied it earlier as part of a Doctor of Ministry degree I'd completed in 1996. The topic of my thesis for this degree touched on the three main understandings of hell in the history of Christianity—those being: hell as a place of eternal torment, hell as a place of final annihilation, and hell as a place of restoration. Once I started looking again into Christian universalism in 2011–2012 I quickly discovered the landscape had changed quite a bit. My previous research had been done in 1996 without the aid of the internet. But this time around, with the help of the internet, I discovered stronger arguments for hell as a place of restoration. And to my complete shock and surprise, I discovered most of the recent writing in favor of Christian universalism was coming from people with backgrounds in the evangelical wing of the church.

I was especially impressed with the book *The Inescapable Love of God* written by a Christian professor of philosophy named Thomas Talbott. In Talbott's work I found another signpost. Talbott wrote at a genuinely academic level and gave insightful arguments for Christian universalism. I was fascinated with the gentle but powerful, logical progression of Professor Talbott's thought. As I continued my research I was also surprised to discover that William Barclay had come to believe God would ultimately save all. Barclay (1907–1978) was professor of divinity at Glasgow University. Barclay's commentary set on the New Testament sold millions of copies and was in the church library of every church in which I'd ever served. Barclay, in *A Spiritual Autobiography*, wrote about how he had come to an understanding of himself as a *convinced* universalist. He gave credit to the early church fathers who had believed this way. But Barclay also wanted to set forth his own reasons on why he had come to this conclusion. He gave four reasons why. First, he thought there was more than enough evidence in the New Testament to support it. Second, he believed the phrase *eternal torment* found in Matthew 25:46 could just as easily be understood in the original Greek to mean *remedial punishment*. His third and fourth reasons had to do with the power of grace and the nature of God. I found his third and fourth reasons especially compelling. Here they are in full:

> Third, I believe that it is impossible to set limits to the grace of God. I believe that not only in this world, but in any other world there may be, the grace of God is still effective, still operative, still at work. I do not believe that the operation of the grace of God is limited to this world. I believe that the grace of God is as wide as the universe.
>
> Fourth, I believe implicitly in the ultimate and complete triumph of God, the time when all things will be subject to him, and when God will be everything to everyone (1 Corinthians 15:24–28). For me this has certain consequences. If one man remains outside the love of God at the end of time, it means that that one man has defeated the love of God—and that is impossible. Further, there is only one way in which we can think of the triumph of God. If God was no more than a King or Judge, then it would be possible to speak of his triumph, if his enemies were agonizing in hell or were totally and completely obliterated and wiped out. But God is not only King and Judge, God is Father—he is indeed Father more than anything else. No father could be happy while there were members of his family forever in agony. No father would count it a triumph to obliterate the disobedient members of his family. The only triumph a father can know is to have all his family back home. The only victory love can enjoy is the day when its offer of love is answered by the return of love. The only possible final triumph is a universe loved by and in love with God.[2]

Barclay neatly summarized the basic arguments about which I had been reading and studying. For Barclay, the determinative factor lay finally in how God should be considered more than a judge or king, but above all as a parent, and how no parent could finally rest easy until all of their children were back home. During this period of renewed study on the possibility of God saving all, I also had a profound spiritual experience. One night I lay awake

2. Barclay, *Spiritual Autobiography*, 67.

in bed pondering all these things. I started wondering how all of this applied to me. How sure was I of my own ultimate salvation? I had yet to face any real tragedy in my own life. I started wondering what would happen if I was to face real tragedy. Was it possible my whole spiritual life might unravel? Might I potentially crack right down the middle? If I somehow got headed towards an unrecoverable situation, would God intervene? How far would God's parental concern for me go? Then I began the following conversation with God in my mind: "God, I'm doing pretty well spiritually right now. I'm even a minister. But what if the wheels fell off? What if the wheels *really* fell off? What if I completely lost it? What if something terrible happened? What if, because of it, I lost my faith? Then what, God?"

That night, as I lay there contemplating how I wasn't bulletproof, I had to admit, given the right series of tragedies, I might just lose it all. And then I had a God moment. I did not hear an audible voice. But the strong impression I received was this: "David, this is not about you having me. This is about me having you." That was a turning point for me. That was the moment I crossed over spiritually into believing I wasn't just partially saved by grace, but completely saved by grace, completely secure in grace—that there was nothing which could defeat God's perfect will for my life. And then I began to see, of course, this couldn't be just for me. If it was for me, it had to be for everybody. It came to me with great force that each and every person is God's dearly beloved child. We are all being saved by grace alone—saved by God's enduring, sovereign, saving presence in each of our lives.

After this revelatory moment, I began a new way of living spiritually. I began to live out of the understanding that I, and everyone else, was eternally accepted and included. I saw each person, including myself, as a flawed person on one level, but on a much deeper level, as a dearly loved child of God, a sheep of God's flock. From this moment on I saw Jesus as the great shepherd who came to save and deliver all his sheep, which is all of us. I stopped trying to do anything spiritually in order to earn, or to secure my salvation. I stopped trying to do anything spiritually for the purpose of increasing my value in the eyes of God. I stopped doing anything spiritually to make God love me more. I resolved for my only spiritual motivation to be a deeper experience of the grace of God which had been carrying me all along, and which I had come to believe would finally carry me and everyone else to perfection in Christ.

It's paradoxical that the person who originally pointed me to C. S. Lewis was a youth minister from a church which taught a strict doctrine of eternal torment. Because it was the writings of Lewis, beginning with The Chronicles of Narnia, which first sparked a hope in me that there might be a truly good God at the center of everything. Lewis, although not a Christian universalist himself, set me off on my own kind of Narnian adventure which led in that direction. In that journey I would run into George MacDonald, whom Lewis considered his greatest spiritual mentor. From George MacDonald I would graduate to modern scholars such as Brad Jersak, Robin Parry, Illaria Ramelli, Thomas Talbott, and David Bentley Hart. In this journey I encountered ever greater signposts which continued to increase my confidence that the judgments of God are ultimately part of the loving grace of God because their ultimate purpose is to accomplish the final healing of the soul. I now know that this understanding of the Christian faith is not new, but as old as the Father of the Fathers, Gregory of Nyssa, and the early centuries of the church. This is how I came to believe the deepest meaning of the Christian faith is that we are all included in God's saving grace—a grace which finally saves all.

Conclusion

> A doctrine of hell needs to make good sense in its place in the biblical metanarrative, the grand story that runs from Genesis to Revelation. I shall argue that when located in the plotline of Scripture, a universalist doctrine of hell makes good sense.
>
> —Robin Parry[1]

We all live inside a story—inside a narrative of some kind. How we understand that story will determine how we live life and what we think about its meaning. Although the Christian story is often told in an exclusive or transactional way (as I have defined those terms here), there is also an inclusive way of telling it in which God desires nothing more than to be with all of us until we are all finally well. When our spirituality is rooted in this powerfully inclusive story, then we can come to God in just the same way as a child who has learned to completely trust his or her loving parents. Then it all becomes an exercise in grace. It all becomes about being strongly drawn to a God of perfect love. The Inclusive/Christian universalist approach tells a good story of a good God who is the perfect parent to all. The story it tells is the story of a God who is rescuing all of us in Christ and who will never give up until we are all safely home.

In the Exclusive/Calvinist approach there is also a story being told. It's the story of a God who does not sincerely desire the salvation of all. It's the story of a God who never even grants the possibility of salvation to some. When our spirituality is rooted in this exclusive story, we live believing that only a limited group of elect people have access to salvation. We wonder about the character of God. Why would God condemn the non-elect when

---

1. Parry, "A Universalist View," 103.

they never even had a chance at salvation? They were born with no hope of it. They died with no hope of it. And then they are punished by being forever rejected through annihilation or eternal torment. If we live in this story then a part of us wonders whether we ourselves will finally be counted among the elect—even as we try our best to live out an authentic life of faith. In the Exclusive/Calvinist approach there's a story being told, but it doesn't seem like a very good one.

There's also a story being told in the Transactional/Arminian approach. In this story God only gives so much help—so much grace—to each person. And then God finally leaves the outcome in their hands. The help God gives by grace is absolutely essential, for there would be no possibility of salvation without it. But God, being all-knowing, is aware that the help given by grace will not be effective in some, or many, or perhaps even most cases. God's rebellious children will inevitably use their freedom to fall to their doom. Born into a world in which their failure is foreknown, they have no more hope of salvation than do the non-elect in the Exclusive/Calvinist approach. If we live in this story, it causes us to wonder about the character of God and to wonder whether we ourselves will finally be counted among the spiritually acceptable.

The story the Arminian approach tells may initially seem better than the story of the Calvinist approach. But once we give it more thorough consideration, it becomes apparent that the doom of the non-saved in the Arminian approach ends up being just as inevitable as the doom of the non-elect in the Calvinist approach. As David Bentley Hart astutely observes, when considering the fate of those not saved in either the predestined Calvinist approach or the free-will Arminian approach, "we find curiously enough that absolutely nothing changes."[2] Both approaches tell troubling stories which not only cause tremendous spiritual anxiety, but also ultimately call into question the goodness of an all-powerful and all-knowing God.

Hopeful inclusivism offers a vast improvement over the way the Christian story is usually told. It allows for a strong hope, even a firm conviction, that God will ultimately save all. In this approach God continues to pursue lost souls after death. Hopeful inclusivists can even assert their belief in the ultimate redemption of all, but with the caveat that it can't be asserted as doctrine. This approach also doesn't generate the level of controversy that Christian universalism does. As such, it is a safe harbor for those who believe that a universal salvation is incredibly likely, even

---

2. Hart, *That All Shall Be Saved*, 85.

infinitely probable, but who cannot affirm it without some reserve. Hopeful inclusivism, while not being Christian universalism per se, uses many of the same arguments, maintains a very strong hope, and affirms the full incorporation of humanity into Christ.

Yet, hopeful inclusivism still leaves us with a problem to resolve. How are we to understand even the remote possibility that there might be some, or even just one, that God will not be able to rescue? If God is all-knowing, God would have known in advance about this problem. If it is the case that some might not be saved, then it's also the case that God *might* bring people into existence without their consent, all the while knowing of their inevitable doom. Hopeful inclusivism is an understandable effort to take a full account of human freedom and to leave room for mystery with regard to whether or not all will finally be saved. But the consequence of hopeful universalism is that it leaves open the possibility of some never being saved. And that creates a problem. For if even one is finally lost, or even *might be* finally lost, this inevitably subtracts from the absolute goodness of God.

If, as a Christian, I am proposing belief in an all-powerful, all-knowing, all-good God, this requires me to clearly affirm an unreserved Christian universalism—what Thomas Talbott refers to as a *necessary universalism* in which, "given the nature of God's love, wisdom, and power, it is logically impossible that his grace should fail to reconcile all sinners to himself."[3] I also find myself compelled to agree with David Bentley Hart's assessment that, "if Christianity taken as a whole is indeed an entirely coherent and credible system of belief, then the universalist understanding of its message is the only one possible."[4] Put simply, if God is all-powerful, all-knowing, and all-good, then God must also be all-saving.

The Inclusive/Christian universalist approach is the only one that fully safeguards the goodness of God. It tells the grandest story. It presents a God absolutely worthy of our highest devotion. It successfully resolves the major theological and philosophical problems which arise with belief in an all-good, all-powerful, all-knowing God. The problem of evil is finally resolved because God allows no evil to take place which is not finally turned towards the good. Hell is made comprehensible because hell is not abandonment to never-ending torment or annihilation, but God's final necessary tactic, regretfully taken in order to bring about the person's full restoration. This spirituality is rooted in the utter goodness of God and in

3. Talbott, *Inescapable Love of God*, 191.
4. Hart, *That All Shall Be Saved*, 3.

each person's God-given acceptance and inclusion. In this approach spiritual growth is not for the purpose of earning salvation or for the purpose of increasing God's love towards us. It's all about learning to trust the God of perfect love who would never leave us abandoned in the first place. In this approach God never brings anyone into existence whom God cannot also bring to a good end. Any evil or sorrow God allows into anyone's life is also something God will ultimately be able to redeem and make right. In this approach we can trust there is absolutely no darkness and no sadness which God cannot finally turn into light and joy. This approach understands grace to be the completely reliable saving presence of God in the lives of every single person.

We all live inside a story. How we understand this story shapes the way we understand ourselves, and God, and the meaning of life. What if we understood ourselves to be living inside a story in which everyone finally comes to a good ending; in which every wrong is righted; in which nobody gets away with anything; in which everyone learns their lessons; in which everyone falls short; in which everyone finds faith; in which everyone is healed; in which everyone's wills are truly set free; and in which everyone is finally saved? What if this is the story in which we are all living? What if grace means that God fully accepts each of us in Christ even *before* we each fully accept Christ in us? If God really is this good, and if in the end, God finally does save every last one of us—now that would be a good story.

Afterword

Over the past couple of decades a surprising number of books, including this one, have been written in support of a strictly Christian understanding of universal reconciliation. Having had the opportunity to read a good many of these books, I can attest to the fact that all of the ones I have read impart the good news of the gospel in fruitful ways. But they also target different audiences and seek to accomplish different goals. And if I had to select just one of them to introduce this whole topic to the ordinary churchgoer in the pew, I would find it extremely difficult to pass over David Artman's *Grace Saves All*. That's in part because this book combines an experienced pastor's ability to articulate a spiritual message clearly, accurately, and persuasively with a pastoral understanding of, and concern for, those who continue to have reservations about the message he delivers. This book also serves as an excellent introduction to some of the most recent literature in support of Christian universalism.

In the book's eighth chapter, which is entitled "My Story," we discover that neither Artman nor his parents were churchgoers during his grammar school days. But when he was in the fifth grade, a beautiful sixteen-year-old young woman, hired as a babysitter, led him to Christ in an all too familiar way: by using the fear of everlasting torment as a means of persuasion. "So, there I was," he writes, "stuck in an odd situation: trapped by a beautiful messenger of a terrifying gospel. I did what any frightened kid might do in my situation. I caved." But in the end, his conversion experience left him "feeling even more vulnerable, confused, and terrified about God," and this lasted into his undergraduate days when a youth minister recommended that he read some C. S. Lewis—at which point, a more mature spiritual quest began. As so often happens with such a quest, the focus of his attention came to rest upon the nature of God's redemptive love for the world: its scope and ultimate success in transforming sinners. He never doubted the biblical narrative concerning the universal scope of God's redemptive love; but like Lewis and many other Christians, he worried that the reality of human freedom opens up the logical possibility, at least, that some free persons might freely overpower God's grace forever and thus separate themselves from the divine nature forever as well. Of course, as many free will theists also acknowledge, the logical possibility of escaping God's love forever, a possibility supposedly grounded in the reality of human freedom, in no way removes the logical possibility that God will successfully reconcile to himself the entire cosmos in the end, including every human sinner. And the latter possibility, some Christians have claimed, opens the door to a hopeful universalism, as it is sometimes called: the idea that we can at least hope (and even pray) for the salvation of all, although without any real certainty in the matter.

Accordingly, in a chapter entitled "Mystery and Free Will" (ch. 6), Artman tackles the whole issue of human free will, of God's ultimate sovereignty in the matter of salvation, and of whether we can affirm something stronger than a vague hope of universal reconciliation. Because several philosophical confusions are apt to muddy these particular waters, I offer below a few suggestions for avoiding philosophical confusion at this point.

First, it is important that all parties to any discussion not confuse a merely verbal dispute, as some would call it, with a dispute over some matter of substance. A verbal dispute typically arises when two conditions obtain: (i) the disputing parties use a crucial term in very different (or even slightly different) senses, and (ii) clarifying these different senses will reveal no real disagreement over a genuine matter of substance. As an illustration, imagine that two persons, A and B, appear to be in a dispute about whether free will could exist in a fully deterministic universe, one in which every event that occurs today is an inevitable consequence of conditions that already existed back in the year AD 1500. Imagine further that A and B are using the term "free will" in two different senses. By "free will" A means "having the power to do what one most wants to do in a given situation," a power that one would not typically have in prison; but by "free will" B has in mind a standard libertarian conception, according to which a person chooses freely in a given set of circumstances only if this person categorically could have chosen otherwise in those very same circumstances. Given that B does not deny that the power to do what one most wants could indeed exist in a fully deterministic universe and A concedes that a categorical power to choose otherwise could not exist in such a universe, we have here no real disagreement at all. What we have instead is only a verbal dispute arising from different uses of the same term, "free will."

Second, it is equally important in such a discussion to avoid *unexplained* (or insufficiently explained) philosophical and theological jargon. Consider more closely the jargon term "libertarian freedom." How much does that piece of jargon, as you understand it, clarify the limits of *possible* freedom? Suppose that a schizophrenic young man should kill his loving mother, believing her to be a sinister space alien who has devoured his real mother; and suppose further that he does so in a context in which he categorically could have chosen otherwise (in part, perhaps, because he worries about possible retaliation from other sinister space aliens). Would you regard this as a genuine instance of moral freedom? If not, then having the power to choose otherwise could hardly qualify as a sufficient condition of *freely* choosing to act in a certain way. Before you can decide whether freely rejecting God forever is even possible, therefore, you will need a much more complete account of the relevant freedom. If moral freedom also requires a minimal degree of rationality of a kind that neither our schizophrenic young man, nor a typical toddler, nor even a dog would presumably have, however causally undetermined some of their behavior might be, then how, one wonders, could the most irrational choice conceivable—a fully informed decision to shut God out of one's life forever—possibly qualify as a free choice for which one is morally responsible?

Finally, it is also important to stress how certain theological and metaphysical contexts collapse the very distinction between possibility and necessity. With respect to any contingent being like you and me, it makes perfect sense to speak both of our possible existence and of our possible nonexistence. But if the Christian concept of God is that of a personal being who exists necessarily or in all possible worlds, then this way of speaking makes no sense at all. For if this being's existence is even possible, then he exists in some possible world; and if he exists in even one possible world, then he exists in all possible worlds. Therefore, if the existence of this being is even possible, then it is necessarily true that he exists. But suppose now that in an effort to avoid the appearance of dogmatism, presumption, and arrogance, someone should propose a "hopeful theism," which includes the idea that the Christian God's existence and nonexistence are both metaphysically possible. The result would be incoherent nonsense. For if God's nonexistence should be metaphysically possible, then there would again be a possible world in which he fails to exist; and if there should be even one possible world in which he fails to exist, then he would not exist in all possible worlds and would not, therefore, qualify as a being that exists necessarily. One cannot grant even the possibility of God's nonexistence, in other words, without at the same time affirming the impossibility of his existence (or the necessity of his nonexistence). And similarly for the belief that neither an everlasting hell nor a final annihilation of some people is compatible with God's essential nature, as revealed in the Bible. Because God retains the same essential nature in every possible world in which he exists, which is every possible world, his essential nature is very different from an ordinary human property like *being married at one time or another*. The difference is that no human exemplifies the latter property in every possible world in which he or she exists; hence, the possibility of getting married in no way excludes the possibility of remaining single throughout an earthly life. But whatever is inconsistent with God's essential nature in one possible world is inconsistent with it in all possible worlds. So no one who believes, as many Christian universalists do, that God's essential nature is utterly incompatible with an everlasting hell can consistently accept even the possibility that some of those whom God has loved into existence will ultimately come to such a horrendous end. The issue here is a simple one of avoiding a blatantly inconsistent set of beliefs, and this carries no implication for any given character trait in the one seeking to maintain a consistent theology; it carries no implication, that is, of great arrogance, on the one hand, or of a genuine meekness and humility, on the other.

In fact, the term "hopeful universalism," as some have used it, may be a bit of a misnomer. For when St. Paul spoke of *hope*—as when, for example, he mentioned his "hope in God . . . that there shall certainly be a resurrection of the righteous and the wicked" (Acts 24:15)—he was not typically endorsing the possibility that the object of his hope might never be realized. To the contrary, his hope in the resurrection expressed his deep conviction and confidence, even his subjective certainty, that this resurrection would most assuredly occur. So given a similar conviction and confidence that "at the name of Jesus every knee will bow, of those who are in heaven and on earth and under the earth, and that every tongue will confess [joyfully] that Jesus Christ is Lord" (Phil 2:10–11), such a hope in no way excludes the metaphysical necessity of this glorious end coming to fruition at some future time. In that respect, the difference between the hope of universal reconciliation and its metaphysical necessity makes little difference, if any, of a practical religious kind.

In any case, for anyone who wants to learn more about why Christian universalism has gained so many adherents in recent decades, David Artman has provided a valuable introduction and source of information.

Thomas Talbott

Professor Emeritus of Philosophy, Willamette University
Author of *The Inescapable Love of God*

Acknowledgments

THIS BOOK IS A product of grace in that everything about it was suggested to me by others. My thanks to the youth minister from the "hell-preaching church" who nevertheless recommended C. S. Lewis to me, and to Lewis himself for first awakening in me a hope that God might be truly good. My thanks to David Friday, my Kappa Kappa Psi band service fraternity pledge brother, for recommending that I visit First Christian Church in Lubbock. My thanks to Neil Pointer and First Christian Church in Lubbock, Texas, for welcoming me with all of my questions and then for encouraging and funding my seminary education, which helped me to see just how many questions there really were.

My thanks to Brite Divinity School at TCU, and to my many professors there, for making me aware of the larger world of Christian thought and theology. My thanks to my denomination, the Christian Church (Disciples of Christ), for allowing each member, and each minister, the freedom to continue to pursue our best understandings of the faith. My thanks to the Christian Churches (Disciples of Christ) where I served in Rogers, Arkansas, Arlington, Texas, and Chicago, Illinois. My thanks to First Christian Church (Disciples of Christ) in Harrison, Arkansas, where I concluded my years of pastoral ministry. I encouraged you to always be growing in your faith, but I was the one who grew and was changed most of all. My thanks to my Sunday School class, the Mustard Seeds, who have allowed me to process my faith with them over the years. My thanks to Tim and Lanette DenHollander for sharing with me their expertise about all things Dutch and Reformed. My thanks to Ken Reeves for being a conciliatory statesman in the church, and to his wife, Debbie, for decorating all of our lives with grace. My thanks to Bob Dodson for putting up with my ongoing theological ramblings. My thanks to Robin Seymore for her expeditious piquant perspicacity. My thanks to Fred Garry, Ron Richardson, John Marseilles, Brad Crawford, Brad Otwell, Peter DeStefano, and Roger Williams for our many stimulating theological conversations. My thanks to Jim Brattin, who, while not sharing my conclusions, nevertheless gave me constructive feedback within the bonds of Christian fellowship. My thanks to my ministerial colleagues Jarret Banks, Ryan Pfeiffer, and Don Morrow for their understanding and affirmation.

My thanks to Rob Bell for writing *Love Wins*, and also for his *RobCast*—those podcasts helped me to have the courage to express my own views. My thanks to Courtney Richards, who emboldened me to finally start submitting my manuscript for publication. My thanks to George Holcomb for helping me not to be afraid to state my true thoughts. My thanks to Doug Reed, for his amazing ministry of grace at Thorncrown Chapel in Eureka Springs, Arkansas. My thanks to Peter Hiett and the Denver Sanctuary Church for organizing the Forgotten Gospel Conference and the Gospel of Relentless Love Conference, where I was able to connect with other similarly minded Christians and to make friends with George Sarris, whom I thank for graciously performing the audio narration for this book. I also want to thank George for his A Door Standing Open Conference, where I was able to visit with Thomas Talbott and Brad Jersak. My thanks to Thomas Talbott for reading and commenting on this manuscript and for contributing the afterword. My thanks to Brad Jersak for being a thought-provoking conversation partner, for giving me the first recommendation for this book, and for writing the book's foreword. My thanks to Robin Parry and Illaria Ramelli for helping us all to better see the history of the Christian hope that all will be saved. My thanks to Wipf and Stock for publishing many volumes which have helped me and for helping me to get this volume in print. My thanks to David Bentley Hart for making us all think deeply, both philosophically and theologically, about what it means to live in the creation of an utterly good God.

My thanks to my mother, Nancy Howes, and my mother-in-law, Marjorie Collier, for your time listening to me, and for your support and encouragement. My thanks to all those too numerous to name here, who have each helped and encouraged me in their own way. Finally, my thanks to my wife, Amy, for going with me on this journey, and for her own scholarship, which exceeds that of mine.

Recommended Reading

The Inescapable Love of God (Second Edition)
by Thomas Talbott

Talbott grew up in an evangelical home. After college, he attended an evangelical seminary and then went on to earn a PhD in philosophy. He is Professor Emeritus of Philosophy at Willamette University in Salem, Oregon. Talbott's book is both biographical and scholarly. Although quite technical and precise, his book is aimed at a general audience. The audio version of the book, narrated by George Sarris, is excellent.

That All Shall Be Saved: Heaven, Hell, and Universal Salvation
by David Bentley Hart

In this unavoidable and challenging book, Hart, a noted theologian, philosopher, and essayist, makes a profound and pointed case that the Christian universalist approach is the only one that finally makes sense out of the Christian tradition. Hart argues persuasively that if God is the good creator of all, God is also the savior of all, without fail.

The New Testament: A Translation
by David Bentley Hart

In this fresh, literal translation Hart allows the reader to encounter the often-jarring prose of the original Greek text of the New Testament. Hart provides a more neutral translation—one which preserves the text's inherent ambiguities and frees it from the influence of previous doctrinal commitments. The footnotes and postscript contain very helpful commentary on a number of important Greek words and phrases which are relevant to the discussion of eternal destinies.

The Evangelical Universalist (Second Edition) by Gregory MacDonald

The author of this book, Robin Parry, wrote the book initially under the pen name of Gregory MacDonald (combining Gregory of Nyssa and George MacDonald). As a teenager, Parry became a Christian in England during a charismatic revival there. He became a school teacher and continued his own personal education to the doctoral level in biblical studies. Eventually he started working in the field of theological publishing. Parry came gradually to his views. He was especially influenced in his thinking by Talbott's *The Inescapable Love of God*. Parry first published his views under the pen name Gregory MacDonald because at the time he was working for an evangelical publishing house and did not want to cause undue problems for his employer. He continues to work in the arena of theological publishing with Wipf and Stock.

A Larger Hope? Universal Salvation from Christian Beginnings to Julian of Norwich by Ilaria Ramelli

This is a condensed, more affordable, and in some ways updated, version of Ramelli's epic one-thousand-page scholarly work *The Christian Doctrine of Apokatastasis: A Critical Assessment from the New Testament to Eriugena*.

A Larger Hope? Universal Salvation from the Reformation to the Nineteenth Century by Robin Parry with Ilaria Ramelli

Robin Parry, with assistance from Ilaria Ramelli, investigates some of the major figures associated with Christian universalism during this time period. Although not seeking to be a formal history, it does provide some excellent help in accurately situating these figures in historical context. Another volume is planned in this *A Larger Hope?* series which will cover the twentieth and twenty-first centuries.

The Christian Doctrine of Apokatastasis: A Critical Assessment from the New Testament to Eriugena by Ilaria Ramelli

This huge work is the ultimate academic resource for a detailed understanding of how the Christian hope of universal salvation developed in early Christianity. The word *apokatastasis* in the title refers to a Greek word found in Acts 3:21. *Apokatastasis* is often translated into English as "the restoration of all things."

Her Gates Will Never Be Shut: Hope, Hell, and the New Jerusalem by Brad Jersak

In this book Brad Jersak does an excellent job of tracing the history of the development of ideas about punishment in the afterlife. Jersak comes from an evangelical background and grew up in what he now calls infernalism. His spiritual journey has taken him towards membership in the Eastern Orthodox church. His book is a good source for an in-depth overview of the Gehenna tradition in Judaism and Christianity ("Gehenna" is the key word translated as "hell" in the New Testament). He concludes his book in Part Three with a hopeful reading of the book of Revelation. The book's title is taken from a passage at the end of Revelation about the gates of the new Jerusalem always being open. Jersak himself is strongly hopeful that God will accomplish the ultimate redemption of all, although he prefers to leave some room for mystery regarding the end of all things.

Universal Salvation? The Current Debate edited by Robin A. Parry and Christopher H. Partridge

This book features Thomas Talbott presenting the case for a Christian view of the salvation of all. Then, as the title suggests, his view is debated by other scholars. At the end Talbott replies to his interlocutors.

"All Shall Be Well": Explorations in Universal Salvation and Christian Theology, from Origen to Moltmann edited by Gregory MacDonald

This book is a collection of scholarly essays which trace the various ways Christian universalism has been approached through the history of Christianity. The introductory essay by Gregory MacDonald (the pen name for Robin Parry) is very helpful as well.

RECOMMENDED READING

The Coming of God: Christian Eschatology
by Jurgen Moltmann

Jurgen Moltmann is Professor Emeritus of Systematic Theology at the University of Tübingen. This book is an example of how a noted theologian works through the doctrine of eschatology—how God's ultimate purposes are finally realized. Moltmann argues in this book that the final consequence of the cross of Christ can only be a universal salvation.

Four Views on Hell (Second Edition) published by
Zondervan, edited by Preston Sprinkle

This book was updated in 2016 by Zondervan, an evangelically oriented publishing house. The second edition of the book includes a chapter by Robin Parry entitled "A Universalist View." The inclusion of the chapter on the universalist point of view by Robin Parry, according to the book's editor Preston Sprinkle, is very significant. In the first edition of this book, published in 1996, there was no inclusion of a Christian universalist view. It's inclusion in the second edition is based on the recognition by the book's editor that Parry's Christian universalist view is an orthodox option for belief, one with which Evangelicals must now grapple. This book is a good overview of the parameters of this discussion.

Perspectives on Election
Broadman & Holman Publishers

Another way to approach the question of how many will be saved is to look at it through the doctrine of election. Thomas Talbott contributes a chapter in this book entitled "Universal Election and the Inclusive Nature of Election." Other authors present contrasting points of view. This book gives a good example of how scholars from various Christian perspectives debate this topic.

Love Wins
by Rob Bell

Rob Bell was at one time an up and coming megachurch pastor in the world of Evangelical Christianity. In *Love Wins* he does not formally endorse a view of universal salvation, but he gives a good enough argument for its possibility that at its publication it set off quite a controversy. His book

RECOMMENDED READING

helped ignite a resurgence of interest around the topic of Christian universalism, and it's become an important contribution to this conversation.

Heaven's Doors: Wider Than You Ever Believed!
by George Sarris

In this very readable book, George Sarris, a conservative Christian, narrates his journey into the belief that God will ultimately save all. He started wondering about the problem of a loving God and an eternal hell in seminary. After doing research on the topic he discovered that universal salvation was a view held in the early church and that there was a solid biblical argument to be made for it. Sarris is a professional Christian actor and communicator, and his book is both engaging and informative. He does an exceptional job of describing how the doctrine of universal restoration was held by many in the early centuries of Christianity.

Flames of Love: Hell and Universal Salvation
by Heath Bradley

Heath Bradley is an ordained elder in the United Methodist Church. His book is a good introduction to the place of universal salvation in Christian theology. Bradley first began thinking in depth about universal salvation at the University of Arkansas when he was pursuing his MA in philosophy. As part of his studies in philosophy he was assigned Thomas Talbott's book *The Inescapable Love of God*. He ultimately found Talbott's arguments persuasive, and he continues to hope and believe in the ultimate salvation of all through Christ. The United Methodist Church does not teach universal salvation. Therefore, Bradley stands in tension with the official teaching of his church.[1]

---

1. For the official position regarding universal salvation and the United Methodist Church see their website at https://www.umc.org/en/content/does-the-united-methodist-church-believe-in-universal-salvation. In footnote 33 in Bradley's book he gives the following explanation of his relation to the Methodist tradition: "Although Christian universalism was not John Wesley's view, and is not the official view of the United Methodist Church, I believe that the kind of Christian universalism outlined in this book can flow organically out of the key convictions of Wesleyan theology, without subverting or distorting any of the key doctrines of the UMC. In my own theological development, it has been Wesley's insistence that love is God's 'reigning attribute,' along with his conviction that love and justice cannot be separated in God, that lead me to explore and ultimately embrace the hope of Christian universalism. On these points, see Jones, *United Methodist Doctrine*, 107; Maddox, *Responsible Grace*, 53" (Bradley, *Flames of Love*, 130, n. 33).

RECOMMENDED READING

*All You Want to Know About Hell: Three Christian Views of God's
Final Solution to the Problem of Sin* by Steve Gregg

Steve is a self-taught Bible student who grew up as a Bible-believing Evangelical. Over time Steve became aware of rumblings within Evangelicalism with regard to doubts about the doctrine of hell as eternal conscious torment. Gregg became aware of arguments within Evangelicalism that God might just annihilate the damned, a much more humane solution. Gregg also became aware of arguments, again arising out of Evangelicalism, that the judgment of God is actually for the purification and restoration of all people. His book is an excellent illustration of how a regular Bible-believing person came to be aware of the problems surrounding the doctrine of hell as eternal torment. Gregg concludes the book undecided as to whether annihilation of the wicked or universal salvation makes the stronger biblical argument, although he does hope universal salvation is true in the end. He does an excellent job of setting out the arguments for all points of view.

*Christ Triumphant: Universalism Asserted as the Hope of the
Gospel on the Authority of Reason, the Fathers, and Holy Scripture
(Annotated Edition)* by Thomas Allin (edited and with an introductory essay and notes by Robin A. Parry, with a foreword
by Thomas Talbott)

Thomas Allin was an English clergyman (1838–1909). His writings on the topic of universal salvation show how a Christian from the 1800s approached these ideas. The extensive historical notes from Robin Parry are extremely illuminating, as is the foreword by Thomas Talbott.

*Razing Hell: Rethinking Everything You've Been Taught about
God's Wrath and Judgment* by Sharon Baker Putt

Putt's book grew out of her experiences teaching religion to collegiate undergraduates. In her book she lays out the reasons one may hope in a universal salvation for all. In the book she leaves open the possibility that some may choose eternal hell even when their souls are freed from all deception. However, she has since made it clear in interviews that she is a Christian universalist.[2] Her view is that once the purifying judgment fires of God finally destroy all unrighteousness, the righteous person, being in their right

---

2. Listen to her interview on the *Nomad* podcast from Great Britain, "Sharon Baker—For the Love of God," 28:15.

mind, will freely choose redemption in Christ. Her book is an engagingly written overview of the topic.

The History of Time and the Genesis of You
by Peter Hiett

Hiett grew up in and then became a minister in a conservative Presbyterian denomination with a strong commitment to classic Calvinist doctrine. His eventual problem with the Calvinist doctrine of limited atonement caused him to have to leave his denomination. However, this led to his founding of the Sanctuary Denver Church. Hiett may have lost standing in the church he grew up in, but he never lost his sense of humor along the way. That sense of humor is apparent in the section at the end of this book entitled "Everything Good and What the Hell?" in which he outlines his reasons for believing God will ultimately make all things new.

Hope Beyond Hell: The Righteous Purpose of
God's Judgment by Gerry Beauchemin

Gerry is a lay evangelical minister. His commitment to a conservative approach to Scripture is clearly evident in his writing. He passionately presents his contention that this point of view is not a departure from Scripture, but what Scripture reveals when read in its original languages and context.

Destined for Salvation: God's Promise
to Save Everyone by Kalen Fristad

Kalen is a now retired United Methodist minister. His book outlines the basic arguments for a Christian vision of universal salvation. Two of the most basic tenets of his faith are that God is unconditionally loving and is all-powerful. In this book Kalen brings together his many years of experience in ministry, and his years of research on the hope that all will finally be saved.

God Is a Gift: Learning to Live in Grace
by Doug Reed

Doug, by temperament, is a perfectionist. Over the years this both fueled his success in ministry and contributed to a difficulty in fully comprehending the meaning of grace. He finally had to learn that God really is a gift. And then he had to learn how to live in grace. For him it was like learning to walk all over again spiritually. His book is a deep reflection on the limitless capacity of grace.

Spiritual Terrorism by Boyd Purcell

Purcell, who eventually became a professional counselor, had to overcome years of exposure to hyper, fear-based Christianity. In the book he examines the effect of continued exposure to literal and legalistic interpretations of the Bible which contain mixed messages about God's love and justice. His book offers a spiritual antidote for those who have been spiritually traumatized by these kinds of experiences.

Grace Beyond the Grave: Is Salvation Possible in the Afterlife? A Biblical, Theological, and Pastoral Evaluation by Stephen Jonathan

Stephen Jonathan's reflections on the possibility of grace beyond the grave grew out of his experiences in evangelical ministry. In the introduction he writes about his struggle to responsibly answer the questions his church members had about this topic. That study eventually led to a large research project. He regards the question of whether there will be an ultimate universal salvation as beyond the scope of his book. His main purpose is just to evaluate the possibility that God continues to pursue lost souls after death for the purpose of salvation. *Grace Beyond the Grave* offers a focused evaluation of this single issue.

Jesus Undefeated: Condemning the False Doctrine of Eternal Torment by Keith Giles

Keith Giles points out how it is that Christians have from the earliest times had three views of hell: eternal torment, annihilation, and universal reconciliation (or patristic universalism). Giles is especially concerned to show the difficulties with the eternal torment view. Beyond that he gives the cases for annihilation and universal reconciliation. He ultimately supports universal reconciliation as the best approach. He makes good use of quotes from early church fathers and gives an impressive summary of quotes from them in an appendix. Giles is especially concerned to show the significance of the destruction of the Jerusalem temple in AD 70.

RECOMMENDED READING

Raising Hell: The Short and Sweet Version; Christianity's Most Damaging Doctrine Under Fire by Julie Ferwerda

Julie grew up in the evangelical church. She began to investigate the possibility of God saving all through Christ when her teenage daughter was considering leaving the Christian faith over the doctrine of eternal hell. In the age of the internet she was able to do a great deal of research on her own. Her book is a good example of how an "average" person with above average determination finds her way to believing that God will finally save all. She has a full-length version of this book as well, but the short and sweet version does a good job of quickly hitting all the highlights of her argument.

Appendix—Lenten Devotional 2018

In March of 2018 I was invited by the minister of a Presbyterian church (PCUSA) to deliver a devotional at a series of mid-week Lenten luncheon services. It is the tradition of that church to invite minsters from a variety of backgrounds to share in these talks. My talk was scheduled to be during Holy Week on the Wednesday before Easter. After the invitation to speak was given to me, I immediately thought that the Presbyterian church would be a good setting in which to thank the Reformed theological heritage of the Presbyterian Church for helping me to see more clearly the importance of the sovereignty of God, as well the understanding that it is grace alone that saves. And then it came to me that I would like to use as my text for the day Jesus' declaration in John 12:32, "When I am lifted up I will draw all people to myself." My talk at the Presbyterian church was video recorded and is available online on YouTube.[1] I include the text of it here because it serves as a good, short explanation of why I believe grace saves all.

However, before we get to the text of my devotional talk, there is one thing about John 12:32 that I would like to clarify. The NIV, ESV, the Good News, and other versions translate the first phrase as, "When I am lifted up." Meanwhile, the KJV, NASB, Young's Literal, and other versions translate the first phrase as, "If I am lifted up." When I gave this devotional talk, the pulpit Bible from which I read had "When I am lifted up." In my own written notes I was not consistent, and I moved back and forth between "if" and "when." I don't know which translation is superior, and it doesn't change my basic presentation too much, but I did want to point it out because others noticed and wondered about it.

---

1. David Artman, "David Artman - Lenten Devotional."

David Artman Lenten Devotional

I want to begin today by saying how honored and humbled I am to be invited to speak here at the Presbyterian Church. I am grateful to the Presbyterian Church for its warmth and its hospitality. I have always felt welcome here, and I have always felt a spiritual bond with the Presbyterian Church. And that bond has strengthened even more so, because the spiritual tradition of this church has lately played an important role in my own continuing spiritual growth and development.

The Presbyterian Church has its theological roots in the Reformed theological tradition, which goes back to John Calvin, and in many ways even further back to the time of St. Augustine in the early church. And there are two parts of this Reformed theological tradition which have become increasingly important to me as I have continued to grow spiritually. But before I get to these two points, let me first say something about spiritual growth.

Spiritual growth is a funny thing. At certain points in your life you can feel so certain that you are right about something, and then later on you can see it a little bit differently. I remember when I was in seminary, coming to the end of my first year. I had been exposed to many of the great questions that had vexed theological minds down through the centuries. And I was visiting with a friend of mine. And I said to him, "You know, just think of all of the complicated theological dilemmas that there are. And after just one year in seminary, I'm right about everything! Isn't that amazing. I mean, what are the odds of that?" With regard to my correctness in all things spiritual I like to say, "I've always been right about everything, but I have changed my mind a few times."

So, with regard to this there are two particular areas the Reformed theological tradition of the Presbyterian Church that have helped me to be right in a different way than I was right before. Now, in my church, the Christian Church (Disciples of Christ), we are each encouraged to come to our best theological understandings and ideas. In our church we like to put it this way, "We have no creed but Christ, and everybody is welcome." So, what I share here are my theological opinions—my deepest understandings of what this means. And so now back to these two parts of the Reformed tradition that have become important to me.

The first area where I've changed my opinion because of the Reformed tradition has to do with the sovereignty of God. Now the sovereignty of God is a major theme in Reformed theology. To speak of God as being sovereign is to speak of the way in which God is finally in charge. After all, we do read in the Bible of a God whom no one is able to withstand (Chron 20:6), who does whatever he pleases (Ps 115:3), whose purpose is established regardless of what plans the human mind may devise (Prov 19:21), whose purposes may not be thwarted (Job 42:2), whose plans always come to pass (Isa 14:24), who declares the end from the beginning and who says, "My counsel shall stand, and I will accomplish all my purpose" (Isa 46:10), who accomplishes all things according to his will (Eph 1:11), for whom nothing is too hard (Jer 32:27), and for whom all things are possible (Matt 19:26).

Because of biblical affirmations such as these, the sovereignty of God is a central theme in Reformed theology. And now it's something that I have learned to receive as good news in my own spiritual life. I used to think I was the one in charge of my eternal spiritual destiny. I used to think I was the one who would ultimately decide where I ended up. But now I have come to rest in the security that it's God who is finally in charge of my spiritual destiny, not me. God is the one driving the ship of my salvation. My only job is to trust. I still have my part to do. But God is with me, encouraging me, nudging me, keeping me moving along. When it comes to my salvation I have come to believe that God is, as they say, "in it to win it"! Coming to rest in the sovereignty of God has allowed me to have peace, because my peace is not in my ability, but in God's. This has allowed me to work hard spiritually, not because I am afraid I will fail, but because I am confident that God's work in me will not fail. The sovereignty of God has become for me security.

Now if the sovereignty of God is the first opinion the Reformed tradition has changed my mind about, the second great thing it has helped me to change my mind on is about the power of grace to save. In the Reformed theological tradition, it is understood that grace alone saves. Grace doesn't just lead part of the way to salvation. It leads all the way to salvation. Because of Reformed theology I now understand better than ever Paul's declaration in Ephesians 2:8, "For it is by grace you have been saved, through faith—and this is not from yourselves, it is the gift of God—not by works, so that no one can boast."

Salvation is not something I am achieving with God. Salvation is something God is achieving with me—by grace alone—through faith alone. Grace is the way God ignited faith in my life. Grace is the way I was born again. Grace is the way God moved in me to give me the new birth from above. As Jesus told Nicodemus that fateful night, "The wind blows where it chooses, and you hear the sound of it, but you do not know where it goes. So it is with everyone who is born of the Spirit" (John 3:8). Grace, like the Spirit, has its own movements and its own schedule. It is not for me to control, but it is for me to cooperate. I am thankful that the Presbyterian Church and the Reformed theological tradition have helped me to see all of this more clearly.

And now, I want to share another spiritual understanding which has become important to me. And it has to do with my text for today, John 12:32. This text is especially appropriate for Holy Week because it has to do with Jesus' understanding of the cross. In John 12:32 Jesus proclaims, "And I, when I am lifted up from the earth, will draw all people to myself." When Jesus spoke about being lifted up he was referring to how he would suffer and die. We know this because in the very next verse, John 12:33, it says, "He said this to show the kind of death he was going to die." So Jesus, referring to the cross, said that if he was lifted up he would draw all people to himself. First, I would turn our attention to the verb which is translated "draw" in this verse. The word translated "draw" is taken from the Greek word *helkuo*. This same word is used later in John's Gospel (John 18) to describe how Peter drew his sword to defend Jesus on the night of his arrest. Even later in John's Gospel (John 21) that word is also used to tell us what Jesus' disciples were doing when they dragged a net full of fish to Jesus.

In John 12:32, where Jesus states his intention to draw all people to himself if he is lifted up, this same verb, *helkuo*, is used. Therefore, when Jesus speaks of drawing all people to himself after being lifted up, he's speaking like a man resolutely drawing a sword, or a like a fisherman straining to drag in a net full of fish. This tells me that Jesus, and by extension God, is intense about drawing me into salvation. And it's not just my salvation God is so intense about. Jesus is determined that if he is lifted up *all* would be drawn toward his salvation.

And this isn't the only place in the New Testament we get this impression. In the New Testament we find Jesus telling a parable about a shepherd who searches for his lost sheep until he finds it (Luke 15:4). We are told in 1 Timothy of a God who desires everyone to be saved (1 Tim 2:3-4). We are informed in 2 Peter about a God who wants none to perish (2 Pet 3:9). We are taught in Romans 5 that the effect of Christ's obedience covered over the effect of Adam's sin. We hear in 1 Timothy of a savior who gave himself as a ransom for all (1 Tim 2:6). And we are advised in 1 Corinthians about a God who will finally be all in all (1 Cor 15:28).

All of this has dramatically expanded the way I now understand the meaning of the cross. When Christ said he would draw all people to himself if he was lifted up on the cross, that speaks to me of God's intense saving will towards all people. And when I combine the intense saving will of God for all people with the Reformed tradition's emphasis on the sovereignty of God and the power of grace alone to save, I come to a powerful vision of the God who saves. I now see Christ on the cross as the beginning of an unstoppable grace—an irresistible one, which is working its way through all of humanity. Little by little, bit by bit, in this age and in whatever ages are still to come—it keeps on working. It may seem to move in weakness, but it's actually moving with tremendous power. In the same way that running water slowly but surely carved out the beauty of these Ozark bluffs and hills, the grace of God is at work, slowly but surely carving out the beauty of each and every person—and ultimately of all creation.

In crucifying Christ, the powers that were trying to stop him actually made him unstoppable. Why am I a Christian? Because by grace Christ has drawn me and is continuing to draw me. There was a time when I would have told you that I didn't want to be a Christian. There was a time when the apostle Paul would have told you the same thing. In his day Paul was Christianity's greatest opponent. But the time came for Paul, and the time came for me, and the time came for you. And if the time hasn't come for you yet, I believe it will come. I believe in a coming time, as Paul puts it in Romans 14:11, when every knee shall bow, and when every tongue shall confess that Jesus is Lord, to the glory of God. And I believe it will all happen by grace.

And so, with the help of the Reformed theological tradition, I have come to see a grand view of the salvation which was unleashed when Christ was nailed to that cross. I have come to believe that when they nailed Christ to the cross they unwittingly unleashed an unstoppable flow of grace and mercy and healing. The greatest stream of healing for humanity was ironically unleashed by the greatest act of violence by humanity. The best man who ever lived was subjected to the worst suffering and death man could ever inflict. Humanity crucified Christ, and Christ responded in love. And that released an immense saving power into the world for the healing of humanity—a loving power that is ultimately irresistible. And that power keeps on drawing us, and keeps on drawing us, and keeps on drawing us. And it doesn't ever stop. And it doesn't ever lose. And, that's the good news. At least in my opinion. But, I do think I'm right.

APPENDIX—LENTEN DEVOTIONAL 2018

Let's pray. Heavenly Father, thank you for coming to us in love. Thank you for continuing to love us even when we turned on you. In Christ you received our violence in love and turned it into an inexhaustible font of healing for the world. And we are eternally grateful. In Jesus' name, Amen.

Bibliography

Artman, David. "David Artman - Lenten Devotional." *YouTube*. April 5, 2018. https://www.youtube.com/watch?v=yjn9N4mKqXA.

Augustine. *Enchiridion on Faith, Hope, and Love*. Translated by Albert Outler, orig. published in 1955. Kindle ed. N.p.: Christian Classics Ethereal Library, n.d.

———. *On Predestination and Perseverance of the Saints*. Kindle ed. N.p.: GLH Publishing, 2011.

Balthasar, Hans Urs von. *Dare We Hope "That All Men Be Saved"?* San Francisco: Ignatius, 1988.

Barclay, William. *A Spiritual Autobiography*. Grand Rapids: Eerdmans, 1977.

———. *The Letters of James and Peter*. New Daily Study Bible. Louisville, KY: Westminster John Knox Press, 2003.

Bell, Rob. "Alternative Wisdom | Part 6—Sheep, Coins, and Sons." *The RobCast*, episode 157. June 25, 2017. https://robbell.podbean.com/e/alternative-wisdom-part-6-sheep-coins-and-sons/.

———. *Love Wins: A Book About Heaven, Hell, and the Fate of Every Person Who Ever Lived*. New York: HarperCollins, 2011.

Bradley, Heath. *Flames of Love: Hell and Universal Salvation*. Eugene, OR: Wipf & Stock, 2012.

Bonda, Jan. *The One Purpose of God: An Answer to the Doctrine of Eternal Punishment*. Translated by Reinder Bruinsma. Grand Rapids: Eerdmans, English translation, 1998.

Brueggemann, Walter. *First and Second Samuel*. Interpretation: A Bible Commentary for Teaching and Preaching. Louisville, KY: Westminster John Knox, 2012.

Christian, Carol, and Lisa Teachey. "Yates Believed Children Doomed: Psychiatrist Says Mom Delusional, Fixated on Sata." *Houston Chronicle*, March 6, 2002.

Dodd, C. H. *The Epistle of Paul to the Romans*. New York: Harper and Brothers, 1932.

Ellis, Paul. *AD70 and the End of the World: Finding Good News in Christ's Prophecies and Parables of Judgment*. Kindle ed. Auckland, NZ: KingsPress, 2017.

Harmon, Steve. "The Subjection of All Things in Christ." In *"All Shall Be Well": Explorations in Universal Salvation and Christian Theology, from Origen to Moltmann*, edited by Gregory MacDonald. Eugene, OR: Wipf & Stock, 2011.

Hart, David Bentley. *The Doors of the Sea: Where Was God in the Tsunami?* Grand Rapids: Eerdmans, 2005.

———. *The Hidden and the Manifest: Essays in Theology and Metaphysics.* Grand Rapids: Eerdmans, 2017.

———. *The New Testament: A Translation.* New Haven: Yale, 2017.

———. "Saint Origen." *First Things*, Oct. 2015. https://www.firstthings.com/article/2015/10/saint-origen.

———. *That All Shall Be Saved: Heaven, Hell, and Universal Salvation.* New Haven: Yale University Press, 2019.

Hatmaker, Jen. *Of Mess and Moxie: Wrangling Delight Out of This Wild and Glorious Life.* Nashville: Thomas Nelson, 2017.

Hazeldine, Stuart. "Does 'The Shack' Teach Universalism?" http://wmpaulyoung.com/shack-teach-universalism/.

Hunsinger, George. *How to Read Karl Barth: The Shape of His Theology.* New York: Oxford University Press, 1991.

Jonathan, Stephen. *Grace beyond the Grave: Is Salvation Possible in the Afterlife? A Biblical, Theological, and Pastoral Evaluation.* Eugene, OR: Wipf & Stock, 2014.

Jersak, Brad. *Her Gates Will Never Be Shut: Hope, Hell, and the New Jerusalem.* Eugene, OR: Wipf & Stock, 2009.

Karlson, Henry C. Anthony, III. *The Eschatological Judgment of Christ: The Hope of Universal Salvation and the Fear of Eternal Perdition in the Theology of Hans Urs von Balthasar.* Eugene, OR: Wipf & Stock, 2015.

Lewis, C. S. *Surprised by Joy.* New York: HarperCollins, 2017.

MacDonald, George. *Unspoken Sermons: Series I, II, and III.* Kindle ed. N.p.: Start Publishing, 2012.

MacDonald, Gregory, ed. *"All Shall Be Well": Explorations in Universal Salvation and Christian Theology, from Origen to Moltmann.* Eugene, OR: Cascade, 2011.

———. *The Evangelical Universalist.* 2nd ed. Eugene, OR: Cascade, 2012.

McClymond, Michael. *The Devil's Redemption.* Grand Rapids: Baker Academic, 2018.

Moltmann, Jurgen. *The Coming of God: Christian Eschatology.* Minneapolis: Fortress, 1996.

Olson, Roger. *Arminian Theology: Myths and Realities.* Downers Grove: InterVarsity, 2006.

———. "Universalism Is 'in the Air' (Much Discussed) among Even Evangelicals: What About It?" Patheos, Jan. 14, 2015. http://www.patheos.com/blogs/rogereolson.

Oppenheimer, Mark. "Evangelicals Find Themselves in the Midst of a Calvinist Revival." *New York Times*, Jan. 3, 2014.

Papaioannou, Kim. *The Geography of Hell in the Teaching of Jesus: Gehenna, Hades, the Abyss, the Outer Darkness Where There is Weeping and Gnashing of Teeth.* Eugene, OR: Wipf & Stock, 2013.

Parry, Robin. *The Biblical Cosmos: A Pilgrim's Guide to the Weird and Wonderful World of the Bible.* Eugene, OR: Cascade, 2014.

———. *Lamentations.* Grand Rapids: Eerdmans, 2010.

———. "A Universalist View." In *Four Views on Hell*, edited by Preston Sprinkle. 2nd ed. Grand Rapids: Zondervan, 2016.

Phillips, Michael. "Introduction." In *Consuming Fire: The Inexorable Power of God's Love; A Devotional Version of Unspoken Sermons*, by George MacDonald, edited by Onesimus. Kindle ed. Charleston: CreateSpace, 2015.

Philo. *Complete Works of Philo of Alexandria.* Kindle ed. Hastings, UK: Delphi Classics, 2017.

Piper, John. *Does God Desire All to Be Saved?* Wheaton, IL: Crossway, 2013.

BIBLIOGRAPHY

Pridgeon, Charles. *Is Hell Eternal? Or Will God's Plan Fail?* Kindle ed. N.p.: Edessa, 2014.

Purcell, Boyd C. *Spiritual Terrorism: Spiritual Abuse from the Womb to the Tomb.* Bloomington: AuthorHouse, 2009.

Putt, Sharon Baker. *Razing Hell: Rethinking Everything You've Been Taught about God's Wrath and Judgment.* Louisville, KY: Westminster John Knox, 2010.

Ramelli, Ilaria. *The Christian Doctrine of Apokatastasis: A Critical Assessment from the New Testament to Eriugena.* Boston: Brill, 2013.

Rohr, Richard. *Everything Belongs: The Gift of Contemplative Prayer.* New York: Crossroad Publishing, 2003.

———. "Hell, No!" Audio CD. Albuquerque: Center for Action and Contemplation, 2014.

———. *Jesus' Plan for a New World: The Sermon on the Mount.* Cincinnati: St. Anthony Messenger Press, 1996.

Samaritans Purse. "Franklin Graham - O'Reilly Factor." *YouTube.* April 29, 2011. https://www.youtube.com/watch?v=WL7C6xyWTNU.

Sarris, George. "A Game-Changer on Hell?" *Engaging The Culture!* April 7, 2016. https://georgesarris.blogspot.com/2016/04/a-game-changer-on-hell.html.

———. *Heaven's Doors: Wider Than You Ever Believed!* Turnball, CT: GWS Publishing, 2017.

Schaff, Phillip. *The Complete Works of the Church Fathers.* Kindle ed. Toronto: n.p., 2016.

Schnelle, Udo. *Theology of the New Testament.* Grand Rapids: Baker, 2009.

"Sharon Baker—For the Love of God, Can We Believe in Hell?" *Nomad* podcast, Feb. 7, 2014. http://www.nomadpodcast.co.uk/nomad-60-sharon-baker-and-razing-hell/.

Smith, Alex. "Jesus' Parable of the Sheep & the Kids." *Reforming Hell,* Dec. 20, 2015. https://reforminghell.com/2015/12/20/jesus-parable-of-the-sheep-the-kids/.

Sprinkle, Preston, ed. *Four Views on Hell.* 2nd ed. Grand Rapids: Zondervan, 2016.

Talbott, Thomas. *The Inescapable Love of God.* 2nd ed. Eugene, OR: Cascade, 2014.

———. "Tom Talbott Reviews 'That All Shall Be Saved.'" *Eclectic Orthodoxy,* Sept. 3, 2019. afkimel.wordpress.com/2019/09/03/book-review-that-all-shall-be-saved.

Ware, Kallistos. *The Inner Kingdom.* Vol. 1 of The Collected Works. Crestwood, NY: St. Vladimir's Seminary Press, 2000.

Wright, N. T. *Surprised by Hope: Rethinking Heaven, the Resurrection, and the Mission of the Church.* New York: HarperCollins, 2008.

Yancey, Phillip. *Vanishing Grace: What Ever Happened to the Good News?* Grand Rapids: Zondervan, 2014.

Young, William Paul. *Lies We Believe about God.* New York: Arita Books, 2017.

www.ingramcontent.com/pod-product-compliance
Lightning Source LLC
Chambersburg PA
CBHW071505150426
43191CB00009B/1422